PAT FRANCIS

ALTARS TO OUR KING OF GLORY

HOW TO ACCESS GOD'S
UNLIMITED GLORY

Guardian BOOKS

Belleville, Ontario, Canada

ALTARS TO OUR KING OF GLORY
Copyright © 2016, Dr. Pat Francis

All Rights Reserved. No part of this publication may be reproduced, stored in a retrieval system or transmitted in any form or by any means—electronic, mechanical, photocopy, recording or any other—except for brief quotations in printed reviews, without the prior permission of the author.

All Scripture quotations, unless otherwise specified, are from the HOLY BIBLE, NEW INTERNATIONAL VERSION ®. Copyright © 1973, 1978, 1984 by International Bible Society. Used by permission of Zondervan Publishing House. All rights reserved. • Scriptures marked NKJV are taken from the New King James Version. Copyright © 1979, 1980, 1982. Thomas Nelson Inc., Publishers.

ISBN: 978-1-4600-0631-3
LSI Edition: 978-1-4600-0632-0
E-book ISBN: 978-1-4600-0633-7
(E-book available from the Kindle Store, KOBO and the iBooks Store)

Cataloguing data available from Library and Archives Canada

To order additional copies, visit:
www.altarstoourkingofglory.com

For More Information:
email: chayil@patfrancis.org
phone: 905-566-1084
fax: 905-566-1154
www.patfrancis.org

Guardian Books is an imprint of *Essence Publishing,* a Christian Book Publisher dedicated to furthering the work of Christ through the written word. For more information, contact:
20 Hanna Court, Belleville, Ontario, Canada K8P 5J2
Phone: 1-800-238-6376 • Fax: (613) 962-3055
Email: info@essence-publishing.com
Web site: www.essence-publishing.com

Printed in Canada
by
Guardian
B O O K S

Altars to Our King of Glory

HOW TO ACCESS
GOD'S UNLIMITED GLORY

Pat Francis

Contents

Introduction 7
Chapter 1: The Power of Altars 11
Chapter 2: Covenant Altars 25
Chapter 3: A Personal Altar 39
Chapter 4: A Family Altar 59
Chapter 5: A Home Altar 69
Chapter 6: A Community Altar 77
Chapter 7: A National Altar 89
Chapter 8: The Church Altar 99
Chapter 9: The Altar of God, the Cross 107
Chapter 10: Altars of Abraham 121
Chapter 11: Altar of Repentance 131
Chapter 12: Altar of Peace 137
Chapter 13: Altar of Intercession .145
Chapter 14: Divine Interventions .153
Chapter 15: Mission INFUSION 169
Chapter 16: The CHAYIL Glory Movement 185

Introduction

In this book you will understand the principle, privilege, and power of building spiritual altars to our King of glory. You will learn about different types of spiritual altars and how Abraham, patriarchs, kings, and priests built altars strategically in times of battles, for family and power covenants, to stop sickness, to break curses, to secure land, and for community and national influence.

You will grow into a greater intimacy with God as your secret dwelling place and your heart His. David prayed, *"Summon your power, God; show us your strength, our God, as you have done before"* (Psalm 68:28), and David's King of glory manifested His CHAYIL glory in and through him, bringing great glory to the God of Israel. God wants to show His glory through His glorified servants. Moses prayed, *"Now show me your glory"* (Exodus 33:18). Not only did Moses see God's glory around him as cloud by day and fire by night (Shekinah glory), but he also experienced God's glory working through him in miraculous power, signs, and wonders (CHAYIL glory). Before Moses' altar of intercession, the Amalekite army was defeated. Now before God's spiritual altars, demons bow, locked-up promises are released, and the glory of the Lord Jesus Christ is filling the earth.

Altars are powerful, and the privilege of building spiritual altars to our King of glory gives us access to realms of glory that are available to all believers in Jesus Christ. When a spiritual altar is built unto God, it creates an open gate, door, or portal into the realm of the spirit, to intentionally be in the presence of the Most High God, for worship, communion, confession, consecration, covenants, prayer, intercession, exchange, offerings, receiving revelation and instructions, and to receive fresh power and glory to go forward in ministry as servants of His manifested glory. It is built by faith for a personal encounter with God for the release of His power, peace, mercy, forgiveness, blessing, and kingdom to rule in our hearts, place, community, and nation. It is to establish the kingdom of God on earth.

Covenant altars are powerful even when built to demons and therefore have generational influence that have to be broken by Christians. There are prayers in this book to ensure that what might have skipped you will not fall on your children. Noah built an ark that caused God to make a vow that as long as the earth remains, He will never destroy the earth by flood again. Altars are powerful. Abraham consistently built altars as he journeyed from country to country, establishing covenant and the blessing of God. Isaac and Jacob continued the tradition of building altars to God after learning from Abraham, their father, the power of altars.

Successful warriors like Gideon, great kings like David, and priests of God built altars by the command of God, for their own personal relationship with God and in times of crisis. Now we do not build physical altars, but the power and principles are still relevant; *"Jesus Christ is the same yesterday and today and forever"* (Hebrews 13:8). Jesus Christ is our *"King of glory, the Lord strong and mighty, the Lord mighty in battle"* (Psalm 24:8). His message to the churches, *"I am the Root and the Offspring of David, and the bright Morning Star"* (Revelation 22:16). The altar that Jesus built for you is still powerful. Now we build powerful spiritual altars to Jesus Christ, our King of glory.

Introduction

CHAYIL glory and Shekinah glory are mentioned in this book. Both *CHAYIL* and *Shekinah* are Hebrew words like the word *Shalom*. CHAYIL glory, unlike Shekinah glory, is the manifested glory of God working *in* and *through* His servants. Shekinah describes the manifested presence of God *with* the people of God as seen with the Israelites as they travelled through the wilderness, *"He guided them with the cloud by day and with light from the fire all night"* (Psalm 78:14).

CHAYIL glory, however, is the manifested power and glory of God *in* and *through* His servants: *"Then the Lord said to Moses, 'See, **I have made you like God to Pharaoh**, and your brother Aaron will be your prophet"* (Exodus 7:1 emphasis added). God empowered Moses with CHAYIL glory to destroy the oppressive forces of His people.

The disciples manifested the CHAYIL (active, powerful) glory of the Lord Jesus Christ working *in* and *through* them. Now this is the glory of all believers in Jesus Christ, *"Christ in you, the hope of glory"* Colossians 1:27.

CHAPTER 1

The Power of Altars

David built an altar to the Lord there and sacrificed burnt offerings and fellowship offerings. Then the Lord answered his prayer in behalf of the land, and the plague on Israel was stopped (2 Samuel 24:25).

The first time the word *altar* was mentioned in the Bible, it was built by Noah:

> Then Noah built an altar to the Lord and, taking some of all the clean animals and clean birds, he sacrificed burnt offerings on it. The Lord smelled the pleasing aroma and said in his heart: "Never again will I curse the ground because of man, even though every inclination of his heart is evil from childhood. And never again will I destroy all living creatures, as I have done" (Genesis 8:20-21).

This altar was so powerful that it still has an effect on our world today. God made a vow because of Noah's altar that He would never again curse the ground because of mankind. God's servants such as Abraham, Isaac, Jacob, Moses, Gideon, Samuel, David and others also built altars to our King of glory.

Abraham built altars wherever he went to establish relationship with God:

> The Lord appeared to Abram and said, "To your offspring I will give this land." So he built an altar there to the Lord, who had appeared to him. From there he went on toward the hills east of Bethel and pitched his tent, with Bethel on the west and Ai on the east. There

he built an altar to the Lord and called on the name of the Lord (Genesis 12:7-8).

A covenant altar is powerful as it affects the destiny and legacy of families for generations. The altar that Abraham built at Bethel established with God that his seed for generations would carry on the legacy of the Hebrew faith. Jacob two generations later was drawn to the same place, Bethel, where his grandfather Abraham had promised him to God for the purposes of God. There Jacob saw in a dream an open heaven with angels ascending and descending to bring his prayer of repentance to God. Jacob was restored in relationship with God and established his own altar there and renamed the place Bethel, as it had been changed to Luz. Altars are powerful for generations.

An altar is very *powerful* because it represents a meeting place and a place of approach for a personal encounter with a spiritual power—God or demons. In this book, our focus is on altars to our King of glory. However, Satan knows the power of altars, and they are used widely for occult practices. Satan is a copycat who knows and uses kingdom law and principles to enslave people for generations. Christians are trained to pray but not trained in kingdom dynamics, and sometimes in ignorance or by default we suffer more than is necessary. Intercession is mediation between kingdoms with Satan as the prosecutor and Jesus Christ as Defender of His family and servants. Legal language and protocol is sometimes needed in intercession as covenants, contracts, vows, and rights have to be considered. Jesus died on the cross to break Adam and Eve's covenant with Satan in the Garden of Eden.

An altar is a place of dedication, consecration, sacrifices, offerings, covenants, vows, contracts, and intercession. In the Bible, we see where altars were built unto God. In other cases, people of different religions built altars unto gods and idols, and the Bible calls it demon worship: *"No, but the sacrifices of pagans are offered to demons, not to God, and I do not want you to be participants with demons"* (1 Corinthians 10:20). Gideon was commanded by God to tear down the altar of Baal built by his father:

> So Gideon built an altar to the Lord there and called it The Lord is Peace. To this day it stands in Ophrah of the Abiezrites. That same night the Lord said to him, "Take the second bull from your father's herd, the one seven years old. **Tear down your father's altar to Baal** and cut down the Asherah pole beside it. Then build a proper kind of altar to the Lord your God on the top of this height. Using the wood of the Asherah pole that you cut down, offer the second bull as a burnt offering" (Judges 6:24-26 emphasis added).

Gideon was instructed not only to tear down his father's altar but to replace it with an altar to our King of glory.

Altars therefore are powerful, as when they are built to our King of glory, our Lord Jesus Christ, they attract the power of God and give God the rights to our families, business, churches, and ministries for generations. Because they are powerful, depending on the spiritual power they were built to, it is good for us to understand the difference of spiritual altars in order to ensure that by ignorance we do not invite spiritual encounters with evil spiritual forces.

ALTARS ARE POWERFUL

In the Old Testament, altars to God were built with stones and wood and later bronze and gold. An altar was a place for sacrifices, offerings, covenants, and for an encounter with God. In the Hebrew language, the word *altar* means "a place of slaughter or sacrifice." When altars were made of stones, God specifically instructed them to use unpolished stones as the stones were not to be worshiped or esteemed: *"If you make an altar of stones for me, do not build it with dressed stones, for you will defile it if you use a tool on it"* (Exodus 20:25). Wood was placed on the stone to create fuel to burn the sacrifice, which was usually an animal or bird. The blood sacrifice at the altar symbolized the punishment of death of an innocent animal receiving the penalty of the sin of the person providing the offering.

The altar was the powerful place where an animal received the full penalty and judgment of God, while the guilty person making the sacrifice received forgiveness, justification, atonement, and freedom from God. The altar was a powerful place for a sacrificial offering, a substitutionary atonement, leading to the great altar called the cross, where Jesus became the sacrificial Lamb of God that was slain for the sins of the world. The cross was a powerful place where the manifested CHAYIL glory of the Lord Jesus Christ conquered death and the grave and paid for the sins of the world with His own blood.

Now under the New Covenant, we build spiritual altars by faith to apply the power and principles of an altar built to worship and honor God. A spiritual altar by faith provides access to the power and glory of our Almighty God, EL CHAYIL, Lord of armies, King of glory, where His blood cries out for vengeance against Satan, his evil kingdom, and his demons. Cain killed his brother Abel, and God visited him with judgment: *"The Lord said, 'What have you done? Listen! Your brother's blood cries out to me from the ground'"* (Genesis 4:10). If the cries of the blood of Abel were powerful to move God to apply a curse to Cain, then the powerful blood of Jesus Christ will move the heart of God to curse all wickedness against His family, Church, and purpose. As we discuss the power and purpose of spiritual altars and the types of spiritual altars, by faith we remember the work of Jesus Christ at His ultimate altar, His cross.

A spiritual altar of intercession is where people come together in unity for prayer, believing that the gathering is actually a meeting place with God: *"Again, truly I tell you that if two of you on earth agree about anything you ask for, it will be done for you by my Father in heaven. For where two or three come together in my name, there am I with them"* (Matthew 18:19-20). When you come in agreement to an altar of intercession, the purpose is to mediate in prayer, fight in spiritual warfare, and make your declarations for yourself, your health, your family, your finances, your church, your nation, etc., according to God's Word. When the enemy blocks your prayers, he is undermining God's Word and negating the power of our Lord Jesus Christ. That is why you are called a kingdom enforcer who is forcefully advancing against opposition to the integrity of God's promises: *"From the days of John the Baptist until now, the kingdom of heaven has been subjected to violence, and violent people have been raiding it"* (Matthew 11:12).

As the patriarchs and priests by faith prayed and offered sacrifices to God at physical altars, we now by faith offer sacrifices of praise, prayers, and intercession at spiritual altars. At spiritual altars, wars are fought, kingdoms are engaged, armies are engaged, and princes can be destroyed or elevated. At Daniel's spiritual altars, the demonic prince of Persia fought an angel of God as Daniel wrestled in prayer. God gave us insight in the spiritual warfare that happens at an altar of intercession. After great resistance for twenty-one days, the angel of God was free to bring a message to Daniel:

> Do not be afraid, Daniel. Since the first day that you set your mind to gain understanding and to humble yourself before your God, your words were heard, and I have come in response to them. **But the prince of the Persian kingdom resisted me twenty-one days. Then Michael, one of the chief princes, came to help me, because I was detained there with the king of Persia.** Now I have come to explain to you what will happen to your people in the

future, for the vision concerns a time yet to come (Daniel 10:12-14 emphasis added).

Please note that the angel armies of Jesus Christ are mightier than the armies of Satan.

Paul received revelation on the demonic hierarchy and level of forces that are engaged in spiritual battles at spiritual altars:

> Finally, my brethren, be strong in the Lord and in the power of His might. Put on the whole armor of God, that you may be able to stand against the wiles of the devil. For we do not wrestle against flesh and blood, but against **principalities**, against **powers**, against the **rulers of the darkness** of this age, against **spiritual hosts of wickedness** in the heavenly places. Therefore take up the whole armor of God that you may be able to withstand in the evil day, and having done all, to stand (Ephesians 6:10-13 NKJV, emphasis added).

As in the kingdom of darkness, God also has hierarchy of angels in armies that are engaged in spiritual battles.

> Then war broke out in heaven. Michael and his angels fought against the dragon, and the dragon and his angels fought back. **But he was not strong enough**, and they lost their place in heaven. The great dragon was hurled down—that ancient serpent called the devil, or Satan, who leads the whole world astray. He was hurled to the earth, and his angels with him (Revelation 12:7-9 emphasis added).

Satan and his demons are still not strong enough against our Lord Most High.

Spiritual altars are powerful in the battle for families, churches, souls, land, resources, nations, and kingdoms. Kings, Daniel, Moses, David, and Esther all battled at natural and spiritual altars of intercession. Through spiritual altars and strategic actions, we have confidence in the outcome:

"Then the seventh angel sounded: And there were loud voices in heaven, saying, 'The kingdoms of this world have become the kingdoms of our Lord and of His Christ, and He shall reign forever and ever!'" (Revelation 11:15 NKJV). EL CHAYIL is Lord of armies, King of glory, our victorious Jesus Christ: *"But thanks be to God! He gives us the victory through our Lord Jesus Christ"* (1 Corinthians 15:57).

SPIRITUAL ALTARS TO JESUS CHRIST

Altars are powerful to approach and to attract spiritual powers. Jesus Christ is referred to in Heaven as the Lamb of God who was slain, now exalted and seated on His throne:

> After this I looked, and there before me was a great multitude that no one could count, from every nation, tribe, people and language, standing before the throne and before the Lamb. They were wearing white robes and were holding palm branches in their hands. And they cried out in a loud voice: "Salvation belongs to our God, who sits on the throne, and to the Lamb" (Revelation 7:9-10).

Jesus Christ the Lamb is worshiped in heaven and on earth: *"In a loud voice they were saying: 'Worthy is the Lamb, who was slain, to receive power and wealth and wisdom and strength and honor and glory and praise!'"* (Revelation 5:12). Because of the powerful work done on the cross, we no longer build physical altars made of stone, kill animals, and offer sacrifices made of created things. We do not make graven images or worship idols as that undermines the purity and power of Jesus Christ, and the Bible calls it demon worship with grave consequences. *"No, but the sacrifices of pagans are offered to demons, not to God, and I do not want you to be participants with demons"* (1 Corinthians 10:20).

Now if we make physical altars or bow to idols or pictures of dead people or man-made symbols of people, angels, or animals, it is considered an abomination by God:

> I am the Lord your God, who brought you out of Egypt, out of the land of slavery. You shall have no other gods before me. You shall not make for yourself an image in the form of anything in heaven above or on the earth beneath or in the waters below. You shall not bow down to them or worship them; for I, the Lord your God, am a jealous God, punishing the children for the sin of the fathers to the third and fourth generation of those who hate me, but showing love to a thousand generations of those who love me and keep my commandments (Exodus 20:2-6).

Altars are now to be *only spiritual* as the approach, prayer, and principles of an altar are very powerful. Our Heavenly Father built an altar called the cross of Jesus Christ to replace the building of physical altars for sin offerings and worship. The stones of ancient altars were replaced by the high place on the hill called Calvary or Golgotha. The wood was the cross on which Jesus died. Jesus, the innocent Lamb, was slain, and His blood was shed for the sins of the world. He died on a cross to break the curse on humanity, and the curse was transferred to Satan forever. *"Christ redeemed us from the curse of the law by becoming a curse for us, for it is written: 'Cursed is everyone who is hung on a tree'"* (Galatians 3:13).

BUILDING SPIRITUAL ALTARS TO JESUS CHRIST

We have the powerful privilege to apply the principles and power of spiritual altars in prayer and worship to God. With the understanding of the work of the cross and Jesus as our sacrificial Lamb, the purpose of an altar and the power of an altar we can move into another realm of spiritual power by faith in the work of the cross, the altar of God. When we approach our King of glory at an altar of worship and intercession, we are intentional and come with specific expectations.

A SPIRITUAL ALTAR TO OUR KING OF GLORY

1. **Spiritual not physical.** *"Yet a time is coming and has now come when the true worshipers will worship the Father in spirit and truth, for they are the kind of worshipers the Father seeks. God is spirit, and his worshipers must worship in spirit and in truth"* (John 4:23-24). You might have a convenient meeting place for prayer and communion with God where you engage in a spiritual altar to our King of glory as a dedicated place. The spiritual altar, however, is not the *place* but the practice (your encounter with God) that creates the altar. A spiritual altar of intercession can be online, on Skype, involving technology as the meeting place. A church that honors Jesus Christ as Savior and Lord is a physical altar where a congregation meets for corporate prayer, intercession, and holy sacraments before our King of glory.

2. **Built by faith not muscles.** *"For where two or three come together in my name, there am I with them"* (Matthew 18:20). We must stay away from worship before idols as it brings generational curses. Past idol worship even in Christian groups must be repented of so that its generational influence is broken: *"Dear children, keep yourselves from idols"* (1 John 5:21).

3. ***Built intentionally.*** *"His intent was that now, through the church, the manifold wisdom of God should be made known to the rulers and authorities in the heavenly realms, according to his eternal purpose that he accomplished in Christ Jesus our Lord. In him and through faith in him we may* **approach** *God with freedom and confidence"* (Ephesians 3:10-12 emphasis added). We intentionally build a spiritual altar to approach our Majesty, King Jesus, to enforce His kingdom and will of God on earth in agreement with us.

4. ***Built for intimacy with God.*** The work on the cross restored our original glory that was given to Adam and Eve, a glory that includes intimacy, communion, and interaction with God. Covered in the blood of Jesus Christ, we can now freely enter into the secret place of God, our Most High, for intimacy where He whispers His secrets in an atmosphere of exchange of love. We serve Him in worship, praise, and honor. He minister to us in love and manifested glory.

5. ***Built with expectations.*** *"But you will receive power when the Holy Spirit comes on you; and you will be my witnesses in Jerusalem, and in all Judea and Samaria, and to the ends of the earth"* (Acts 1:8). Our expectation will determine manifestation. We must activate our faith to our King of glory with more of His power and glory to manifest in and through us: *"I have given them the glory that you gave me, that they may be one as we are one"* (John 17:22). CHAYIL glory is the manifested power and glory of our Lord Jesus Christ *in* and *through* His servants. People must see and hear that we are Christians, carriers of the Christ in us, the hope of glory for the world.

6. ***Built for the exchange.*** Our sins are placed at the spiritual altar to Jesus Christ in exchange for His mercy

and forgiveness. Our weakness is placed on the spiritual altar to Jesus Christ in exchange for His power and glory to serve Him. We serve Him in worship in exchange for His scepter of honor. We forgive others at the spiritual altar to Jesus Christ in exchange for His forgiveness. *"For if you forgive men when they sin against you, your heavenly Father will also forgive you. But if you do not forgive men their sins, your Father will not forgive your sins"* (Matthew 6:14-15). *"And when you stand praying, if you hold anything against anyone, forgive him, so that your Father in heaven may forgive you your sins"* (Mark 11:25). The exchange of forgiveness is a powerful privilege for us to remain in freedom for the blessings of God.

7. **Built for intercession.** Intercession is to mediate or intervene for another. With God's power, authority, and the keys of His kingdom that are given to us, we have the power and authority like a lawyer or judge to influence the freedom and outcome of lives and circumstances: *"And I tell you that you are Peter, and on this rock I will build my church, and the gates of Hades will not overcome it. I will give you the keys of the kingdom of heaven; whatever you bind on earth will be bound in heaven, and whatever you loose on earth will be loosed in heaven"* (Matthew 16:18-19). At a spiritual altar, you can pray and intercede as God's kingdom enforcer, that His will is not hindered in our lives or households, in the lives of others, in His Church, or in our world.

8. **Built for kingdom revelation and government.** At the spiritual altar, God reveals His secrets, training, strategies, insights, wisdom, and instruction for follow through. *"He told them, 'The secret of the kingdom of God has been given to you. But to those on the outside*

everything is said in parables'" (Mark 4:11). To know the secrets of God and to have God as your personal coach is an amazing privilege: *"So then, men ought to regard us as servants of Christ and as those entrusted with the secret things of God"* (1 Corinthians 4:1). At the spiritual altar, the government and kingdom of God is established, with Jesus as our King of glory. The power of His presence in our hearts, homes, communities, and nations subdues evil influence and in communities establishes His kingdom. When we set up community spiritual altars in schools and workplaces, we provide a legal ground for His kingdom to be established for "**Mission INFUSION.**" His plan is to infuse His glory in every heart, home, community, and nation. The angels' declaration shall be a reality: *"And they were calling to one another: 'Holy, holy, holy is the Lord Almighty; the whole earth is full of his glory'"* (Isaiah 6:3).

9. **Built by faith declaration.** *"You will also declare a thing, And it will be established for you; So light will shine on your ways"* (Job 22:28 NKJV). We know what we are doing, we say what we are doing, and we expect results. We build spiritual altar for an encounter with God for natural results. By faith, we bring our requests, covenant, vows, offerings, and declarations to our King of glory for His covenant blessing and the release of His power to co-create with us the results: *"Now faith is the substance of things hoped for, the evidence of things not seen"* (Hebrews 11:1 NKJV).

When an altar is made unto Jesus Christ, it establishes His presence, power, mercy, government, kingdom, and blessing to rule in that heart, home, school, workplace, community, and nation. With the *infusion* of the presence of Jesus in communities, demonic powers will bow and be neutralized and hearts and lives will become free to unite to the true and living

Savior of the world, Jesus Christ. Abram built an altar unto Jehovah, the Most High God, as an intentional, physical act symbolizing that the presence of God was now summoned in that land to establish His kingdom, sovereign rule, and priesthood and that God would be worshiped there for generations. *"The Lord appeared to Abram and said, 'To your offspring I will give this land.' So he built an altar there to the Lord, who had appeared to him"* (Genesis 12:7).

When you build a spiritual altar to our King of glory and make a declaration for His kingdom and presence to come and be established in your worship, He comes in His power for manifested glory. *"Your kingdom come, your will be done on earth as it is in heaven"* (Matthew 6:10). By faith, His presence is established in hearts, communities, and nations for His mercy (forgiveness), peace (salvation), power (for transformation), and for His kingdom to come and rule in that land. David prayed, *"Summon your power, God; show us your strength, our God, as you have done before"* (Psalm 68:28). The words *power* and *strength* in the Hebrew language are CHAYIL. You are made in the image of God to speak like God words of faith to create and rule your world.

Abram and his family would meet with God at the spiritual altar for continued relationship, blessings, peace, and prosperity in all their undertakings. Often God manifested His power and glory at the altar with fire, smoke, miracles, and revelations. Expectation is the mother of miracles. What you expect will manifest, and what you believe you will receive.

When you leave the place of a spiritual altar of worship and intercession, leave with God's blessing, power, and glory to serve Him. CHAYIL glory is the manifested power and glory of our Lord Jesus Christ *in* and *through* His servants. The disciples left the upper room with activated CHAYIL glory, and they immediately began to manifest God's glory in wisdom, teaching, miracles, new abilities, and the salvation of thousands of people. A spiritual altar to our King of glory is a place of worship and intercession; spiritual and not physical; built by faith and not by muscles; built intentionally; built for intimacy with God; built with expectations; built for exchange; built for intercession; built for kingdom revelation and government; and built by faith declaration.

CHAPTER 2

Covenant Altars

So if the Son sets you free, you will be free indeed (John 8:36).

Now that we know the power of spiritual altars, it is also important for us to understand the power of *covenant altars* as they are often built in the occult world to tie up generations for the legacy of occult influence. In Numbers 23 we see where Balak, son of the king of Moab, offered to pay Balaam, the prophet of Israel, a great sum of money to put a curse on Israel. The king knew that Israel's covenant protection and power was too great for him to conquer them in battle. Balaam told the king of Moab to build seven altars while he sought an answer from God.

> Balaam said to God, "Balak son of Zippor, king of Moab, sent me this message: 'A people that has come out of Egypt covers the face of the land. Now come and put a curse on them for me. Perhaps then I will be able to fight them and drive them away.'" But God said to Balaam, "Do not go with them. You must not put a curse on those people, because they are blessed" (Numbers 22:10-12).

Notice the negotiations in the spirit world as Satan tried to find legal grounds to put a curse on God's people. What is interesting in this story is that Balaam was a prophet of Israel and yet because of greed, monetary gain, and lust for power he was willing to use his special gift (to bless or curse) even on his own people. This shows that spiritual leaders can be corrupted to operate with both God and satanic powers. The love and the lust for money and power remains the root of all evil.

The king of Moab, who saw the greed in Prophet Balaam, went to him several times with greater and greater bribes, altars, and sacrifices for Balaam to ask God's permission to curse Israel. God even used Balaam's donkey, who was wiser than the man of God, to warn him of his danger, but the lust of the flesh and the pride of life so controlled him that he kept going back to God and then opening up his mouth to see if a curse could be uttered. Every time he opened his mouth to prophesy against Israel, a blessing came out, and they became stronger and stronger because whom God blesses no one can curse.

Balaam could not curse Israel as there were no legal grounds. Unfortunately, however, he figured out a way to still get a reward through counseling the king of Moab about the kingdom dynamics of a curse caused by the actions and sins of a person, family, or nation. He advised the Moabites how to entice the Israelites with sexual immorality and idolatry so that they would put a curse upon themselves. Balak followed through, and Israel began worshiping the Baal of Peor and became involved with sexual sins and perversion, resulting in the death of many Israelites: *"But those who died in the plague numbered 24,000"* (Numbers 25:9).

The kingdoms of the spirit world have religious, legal, and monetary systems that affect generations. An altar creates an open door or portal to realms of the spirit world for connection with either the kingdom of Satan or the kingdom of God. An altar is a place of surrender to spiritual powers to receive power, authority, and influence. Satan is a source of power for his agenda is to steal, kill, and destroy lives and our world. God is a source of power to save, heal, and love the world. Demonic covenant altars involve making an agreement, covenant, vow, or contract with the devil that includes the spiritual legal rights to influence or possess descendants or offspring for generations. Satan understands the laws of the kingdoms in the spirit world. God binds Himself to the spiritual laws of the kingdoms and therefore sacrificed His Son Jesus Christ, with His blood shed on the cross, for all the sins of the world.

The Bible talks about the effects of idolatry, generational sins, and iniquities:

> And he passed in front of Moses, proclaiming, "The Lord, the Lord, the compassionate and gracious God, slow to anger, abounding in love and faithfulness, maintaining love to thousands, and forgiving wickedness, rebellion and sin. **Yet he does not leave the guilty unpunished; he punishes the children and their children for the sin of the fathers to the third and fourth generation**" (Exodus 34:6-7 emphasis added).

Once we become a Christian, the powerful blood of Jesus Christ can break all covenants, contracts, vows, and agreements made by our ancestors.

> For you know that it was not with perishable things such as silver or gold that you were redeemed from the empty way of life handed down to you from your forefathers, but with the precious blood of Christ, a lamb without blemish or defect (1 Peter 1:17-19).

The power of the cross reverses curses. Whatever Satan does can be negated, neutralized, and destroyed by the power of Jesus Christ, by His blood, by His Word, by His name, and by faith in the cross of Jesus Christ. Satan is mighty, but only God is Almighty. God is the Most High, King of kings, Lord of lords, King of glory, and Alpha and Omega. EL CHAYIL is Lord of armies, King of glory, Lord of wealth.

Covenant altars to our King of glory are powerful, as we will see with Abraham and his covenant altars for his offspring for generations.

The Lord appeared to Abram and said, "To your offspring I will give this land." So he built an altar there to the Lord, who had appeared to him. From there he went on toward the hills east of Bethel and pitched his tent, with Bethel on the west and Ai on the east. There he built an altar to the Lord and called on the name of the Lord (Genesis 12:7,8).

Note that God wants to save people for generations. When God called Abraham, He had David, Jesus, and the Church of Jesus in mind. God is Alpha (beginning) and Omega (ending).

THE POWER OF A COVENANT ALTAR TO OUR KING OF GLORY

1. God will keep His covenant with you and show mercy when needed: *"Therefore know that the Lord your God, He is God, the faithful God who keeps covenant and mercy for a thousand generations with those who love Him and keep His commandments"* (Deuteronomy 7:9 NKJV).
2. It establishes covenants and rights to blood and family line.
3. It establishes and propels generational blessings.
4. It gives God the legal rights to influence your children and grandchildren.
5. It opens gates and portals to realms of the spirit and the throne of God.
6. It is a place of surrender to God for ownership of your heart and family lineage for generations.
7. It determines the destiny and legacy of descendants for generations.
8. It is to intentionally establish God's presence for His mercy, power, peace, government, and rule in your life for generations.

9. God is known.

A spiritual covenant altar to our King of glory, the Lord Jesus Christ, is therefore powerful for generations as is the power of Abraham's covenant altar. Abraham's covenant altar had influence on Jacob, his grandson, three generations later.

GOD'S COVENANT PROMISE TO ABRAHAM

The Lord said to Abram after Lot had parted from him, "Lift up your eyes from where you are and look north and south, east and west. All the land that you see I will give to you and your offspring forever. I will make your offspring like the dust of the earth, so that if anyone could count the dust, then your offspring could be counted. Go, walk through the length and breadth of the land, for I am giving it to you." So Abram moved his tents and went to live near the great trees of Mamre at Hebron, where he built an altar to the Lord (Genesis 13:14-18).

Abraham sealed his covenant by building a covenant altar. The covenant altar would affect the destinies of his family for generations. God was named the God of Abraham: *"The nobles of the nations assemble as the people of the God of Abraham, for the kings of the earth belong to God; he is greatly exalted"* (Psalm 47:9).

GOD'S COVENANT PROMISE TO ISAAC

From there he [Isaac] went up to Beersheba. That night the Lord appeared to him and said, "I am the God of your father Abraham. Do not be afraid, for I am with you; I will bless you and will increase the number of your descendants for the sake of my servant Abraham." Isaac built an altar there and called on the name of the Lord. There he pitched his tent, and there his servants dug a well (Genesis 26:23-25).

Almost word for word, God repeated the covenant promises to Isaac that he had made with Abraham. Isaac sealed his covenant with a covenant altar for generations. God changed His name to the God of Abraham and Isaac. *"There above it stood the Lord, and he said: 'I am the Lord, the God of your father Abraham and the God of Isaac. I will give you and your descendants the land on which you are lying'"* (Genesis 28:13).

GOD'S COVENANT PROMISE TO JACOB

Jacob left Beersheba and set out for Haran. When he reached a certain place, he stopped for the night because the sun had set. Taking one of the stones there, he put it under his head and lay down to sleep. He had a dream in which he saw a stairway resting on the earth, with its top reaching to heaven, and the angels of God were ascending and descending on it. There above it stood the Lord, and he said: "I am the Lord, the God of your father Abraham and the God of Isaac. [Note that God did not include Jacob in His name until Jacob established his personal relationship with Him by building a covenant altar.] I will give you and your descendants the land on which you are lying. Your descendants will be like the dust of the earth, and you will spread out to the west and to the east, to the north and to the south. All peoples on earth will be blessed through you and your offspring. I am with you and will watch over you wherever you go, and I will bring you back to this land. I will not leave you until I have done what I have promised you" (Genesis 28:10-15).

Again, almost word for word, the covenant promise to Abraham was the same for Isaac and now for Jacob. *"Early the next morning Jacob took the stone he had placed under his head and set it up as a pillar and poured oil on top of it. He called that place Bethel, though the city used to be called Luz"* (Genesis 28:18-19). Jacob sealed his covenant with a covenant altar for generations.

The power of Abraham's covenant altars affected Jacob, his grandson, who was running for his life and just happened to lie down exhausted to sleep at Bethel, Abraham's place of covenant. Jacob, after agreeing to God's covenant, renamed the place (Luz) back to the name Bethel, the name in his grandfather's covenant. Bethel meant "a holy place." There he had an encounter with God and his eyes were opened to see in a vision angels ascending and descending from there to Heaven. Bethel still had an open portal or gate to Heaven as was established by Abraham. God changed His name again: *"Then he said, 'I am the God of your father, the God of Abraham, the God of Isaac and the God of Jacob,' At this, Moses hid his face, because he was afraid to look at God"* (Exodus 3:6). God was now the God of Abraham, Isaac, and Jacob.

Here we see that covenant altars have influence on generations with the deity or demonic power that they were made to. Idolatry brings generational curses:

> I am the Lord your God, who brought you out of Egypt, out of the land of slavery. You shall have no other gods before me. You shall not make for yourself an idol in the form of anything in heaven above or on the earth beneath or in the waters below. You shall not bow down to them or worship them; for I, the Lord your God, am a jealous God, punishing the children for the sin of the fathers to the third and fourth generation of those who hate me, but showing love to a thousand [generations] of those who love me and keep my commandments (Exodus 20:2-6).

When we speak about building altars in this book, they are always spiritual altars, not made with any physical materials. Our worship is in spirit and in truth, *"God is spirit, and his worshipers must worship in spirit and in truth"* (John 4:24).

BUILDING A COVENANT ALTAR TO THE LORD JESUS CHRIST

1. ***Believe in Jesus.*** *"They replied, 'Believe in the Lord Jesus, and you will be saved—you and your household'"* (Acts 16:31). When you believe in Jesus Christ and receive Him as your personal Savior and Lord, you are transferred into His kingdom and into His royal family and into His Church as a part of His believers.

2. ***Confess your belief in Him.*** Do not hide your relationship with Jesus Christ, unless it is a danger to your life. *"That if you confess with your mouth, 'Jesus is Lord,' and believe in your heart that God raised him from the dead, you will be saved. For it is with your heart that you believe and are justified, and it is with your mouth that you confess and are saved. As the Scripture says, 'Anyone who trusts in him will never be put to shame'"* (Romans 10:8-11).

3. ***Confess all your sins, transgressions, and iniquities.*** *"If we claim to be without sin, we deceive ourselves and the truth is not in us. If we confess our sins, he is faithful and just and will forgive us our sins and purify us from all unrighteousness"* (1 John 1:8-9).

4. ***Obey Jesus and be water baptized.*** *"Whoever believes and is baptized will be saved, but whoever does not believe will be condemned"* (Mark 16:16).

Water baptism can also break personal covenants, contracts, and vows with Satan and establish covenant with Jesus Christ for His eternal blessing.

5. ***Obey God by pursuing a godly lifestyle.*** *"What shall we say, then? Shall we go on sinning so that grace may increase? By no means! We died to sin; how can we live in it any longer?"* (Romans 6:1-2). Avoid the temptation of hypocrisy. When we become saved, we do not become a perfect person instantaneously, but we become a work in progress in an environment of discipleship and strong Christian support. Important, however, is our intention and desire to live a life that is pleasing to God. *"Therefore do not let sin reign in your mortal body so that you obey its evil desires. Do not offer the parts of your body to sin, as instruments of wickedness, but rather offer yourselves to God, as those who have been brought from death to life; and offer the parts of your body to him as instruments of righteousness. For sin shall not be your master, because you are not under law, but under grace"* (Romans 6:11-14).

6. ***Find and join a church.*** Find a church that teaches strong Christian principles and provides strong support to new Christians for your continued growth. Jesus is the Bishop and Ruler of His Church, and He will lead you to the right church where you can grow stronger and stronger in Christ.

7. ***Learn how to grow in Christ.*** Learn how to strengthen yourself daily with worship, prayer, confession, thanksgiving, and praying for yourself and others. Build your personal altar, as outlined in this book. Read and study your Bible. Stay connected to the Body of Christ.

8. Stay covered in Christ. Jesus has placed a covering of His powerful blood that was shed on the cross for you. He has also created for you a spiritual armor for your protection. Read Ephesians 6:10-18, which teaches about the full armor of Jesus Christ.

PRAYER FOR COVENANT WITH JESUS CHRIST

Dear Jesus, I believe in You and receive You as my Savior and Lord. Forgive me of all my sins, mistakes, and failures. I renounce all previous idolatry and profess to serve You only as my God, Lord and King. Come into my heart to rule my world. I declare that my heart is an altar for Jesus Christ alone, built by faith to intentionally establish His presence for His mercy, peace, power, government, and rule in my heart and life for generations. In Jesus' name, I pray. Amen.

SPIRITUAL COVENANTS

Covenants can be made and affect you either by default, ignorance, or intention. A covenant is described as an agreement between two people. In the spirit world, covenants are made between a person or people and spiritual powers. A covenant usually requires a seal, a token, or intentional actions to prove commitment. In marriage, a ring is used as a symbol of covenant and vows are made with witnesses. With an increase in the influence of the occult in schools, the media, etc., covenants can be made ignorantly and foolishly with friends, through games, or through experimenting with demons. *"To the Jews who had believed him, Jesus said, 'If you hold to my teaching, you are really my disciples. Then* you will know the truth, and the truth will set you free'" (John 8:31-32).

PRAYERS FOR BREAKING SPIRITUAL CONTRACTS

Renouncing ungodly covenants and vows

Heavenly Father, in the name of Jesus, I repent and renounce all covenants, contracts, rituals, and vows that I have made with demons and demonic influences. I renounce and repent of praying to or worshiping spirits of the dead (necromancy) in saints, family members, and any religious activities that involve rituals or celebrations for the dead. I renounce and repent of all activities, games, addictive drugs, drinks, and demonic communions and all experiments and participation with demons and the kingdom of Satan.

I realize that it was a mistake on my part to engage in such activities that opened the doors to demonic influences in my life, and I ask You to forgive me and release me from any claims and bondage that are still binding and influencing my life.

In the name of Jesus, by the power of His blood and according to His Word, I now renounce all covenants, contracts, rituals, and vows that I made, even those that are no longer in my memory, involving the satanic kingdom.

In the name of Jesus, by faith, I believe, confess, and declare that I am released and set free by Jesus, Son of the Living God.

By the power of Jesus Christ, by the power of His name, by the power of His blood, and by the power of His Word, I now command all evil spirits that have influenced and taken advantage of unholy covenants, contracts, and vows to leave me now in the name of Jesus!

Heavenly Father, I thank You for the power in the name of Jesus Christ.

Holy Spirit, I ask You to fill me with Your holy power and to break all powers of darkness in my life.

Lord Jesus, I thank You for my deliverance and freedom as I believe that whom the Son sets free is free indeed. Amen!

Breaking generational curses

In the name of Jesus, I repent and confess to the sins, transgressions, and iniquities of my parents, grandparents, and all previous ancestors [name specific sins, generational tendencies, and evil practices known].

In the name of Jesus, by the power of His blood, and according to His Word, I now loose myself and my future descendants from any bonds, ties, and covenants passed down to me by my ancestors.

By the power of Jesus Christ, by the power of His name, by the power of His blood, and by the power of His Word, I now command all evil spirits that have influenced me because of the cords of iniquity, generational curses, and unholy soul ties to leave me now in the name of Jesus!

Heavenly Father, I thank You for the power in the name of Jesus Christ.

Holy Spirit, I ask You to fill me with your holy power and to break all powers of darkness in my life.

Lord Jesus, I thank You for my deliverance and freedom as I believe that whom the Son sets free is free indeed. Amen!

Breaking soul ties

Heavenly Father, in the name of Jesus, I confess and repent of my sins that bound me to an evil soul tie with _____. [Name the person and sins, such as adultery, fornication, sexual sins, exposing them to the light of Jesus for His blood to break the ties.]

Repentance actions: get rid of covenant gifts or objects, such as rings and gifts given in adultery and unhealthy addictive relationships. Break, throw out, burn, or get rid of such objects to show your resolve to be free from all ties.

In the name of Jesus, by the power of His blood, and according to His Word, I now renounce, break, and sever all unholy soul ties formed between _____ [name the person] and myself, through the sin of _____ [name the sinful acts].

By the power of Jesus Christ, by the power of His name, by the power of His blood, and by the power of His Word, I now command all evil spirits that have influenced me because of the unholy soul ties to leave me now in the name of Jesus!

FAITH DECLARATIONS FOR CONTINUED FREEDOM:

* I am forgiven and cleansed by the blood of Jesus Christ.
* I am free in Jesus' name.
* I have been crucified with Christ and I no longer live, but Christ lives in me.
* I am covered by the blood of Jesus Christ.
* I am protected by the full armor of Jesus Christ.
* Christ in me is my hope of glory.
* Greater is Christ in me than he who is in the world.
* I am blessed and highly favored.
* Jesus is my light and my salvation, I will fear no evil.
* No one will be able to stand against me all the days of my life for my God is always with me.
* No weapon formed against me shall prosper, and every tongue that rises against me in judgment shall be condemned.

* I am more than a conqueror through Him who loves me.
* I am convinced that nothing or no one will be able to separate me from the love of God that is in Christ Jesus my Lord.
* I am strong in the Lord and in His mighty power.
* I have the peace of Jesus Christ. I will not let my heart be troubled, and I will not be afraid.
* I will fight the good fight of faith and take hold of the eternal life to which I am called.
* The peace of God, which transcends all understanding, will guard my heart and my mind in Christ Jesus.

CHAPTER 3

A Personal Altar

Isaac built an altar there and called on the name of the Lord (Genesis 26:25).

A *personal altar*, as the name implies, is a personal meeting time with God, one-to-one, for worship, cleansing, Bible study, meditation, sharing of the heart, receiving instructions, receiving fresh glory, and thanksgiving. For some, their personal altar is at a special quiet place and time where they will be undisturbed and find it easier to focus on and honor the presence of God. For others who work in shifts, it is a daily meeting with God whenever and wherever it is convenient. A personal altar is not necessarily a physical place, but it is a secret place near to the heart of God that He has reserved for you. Our worship at the personal altar is in spirit (our hearts connecting with the Spirit of God) and in truth (with a pure agenda to glorify God in His presence and with our lives). The key is to practice the presence of God as a priority at your wake-up time for your personal altar time with God. *"In the morning, O Lord, you hear my voice; in the morning I lay my requests before you and wait in expectation"* (Psalm 5:3).

THE PRIVILEGE OF HIS PRESENCE

"Ascribe to the Lord the glory due his name; worship the Lord in the splendor of his holiness" (Psalm 29:2). Under the Old

Covenant, only the high priest could go into the presence of God in what was called the "Holy of Holies" in the tabernacle or temple. Even so, the high priests were only allowed to be in God's presence on the Day of Atonement. The holy presence of God was regarded as most sacred or special, and it is therefore a great privilege for us now, because of the work of Jesus on the cross, to have free access at any time and any day to the holy presence of God. This privilege was given to us by invitation: *"God, who has called you into fellowship with his Son Jesus Christ our Lord, is faithful"* (1 Corinthians 1:9). God has invited us to intimacy with Him for sweet communion and fellowship. We have an open invitation to come before our Holy God at any time, anywhere, and any day: *"Let us therefore come boldly to the throne of grace, that we may obtain mercy and find grace to help in time of need"* (Hebrews 4:16 NKJV). We might not get the opportunity to meet earthly kings and great leaders, but we have the great privilege to be in the presence of the King of kings and Lord of lords at His personal invitation.

DAVID'S PERSONAL ALTAR

David was a man who was highly exalted by God, and among his many characteristics we can see the practice, power, passion, and fruit of his personal altar. He was described by God with high honor: *"After removing Saul, he made David their king. He testified concerning him: 'I have found David, son of Jesse, a man after my own heart; he will do everything I want him to do'"* (Acts 13:22). David was "after" God's heart, in pursuit of God's heart, mind, will, principles, purpose, nature, and glory. To be "after" God suggests "passionate pursuit," which means an intentional priority to spend time with God, to study about God, and to nurture great intimacy with God. David tapped into a realm with God that no one else did.

A Personal Altar

Jesus boasted in His relationship with David: *"I, Jesus, have sent my angel to give you this testimony for the churches. I am the Root and the Offspring of David, and the bright Morning Star"* (Revelation 22:16). It is good then for us to peek into David's personal altar time with God to hear how he worshiped, prayed, asked for mercy, communed, and nurtured such great intimacy with God.

* **David prioritized communion with God.** He prayed during his personal altar, *"O God, you are my God, earnestly I seek you; my soul thirsts for you, my body longs for you, in a dry and weary land where there is no water"* (Psalm 63:1). David was openly passionate about his adoration and longing for God. David not only loved God, but he was God's lover. His love for God was intentional and determined even in this declaration: *"I will praise you, O Lord, with all my heart; I will tell of all your wonders. I will be glad and rejoice in you; I will sing praise to your name, O Most High"* (Psalm 9:1-2). David did not just think about communing with God, he said and did it. David had several personal altar times and remained open to receiving revelation at any time: *"Evening, morning and noon I cry out in distress, and he hears my voice"* (Psalm 55:17). David remained in sync with God. Even in the night, David practiced listening to God: *"I will praise the Lord, who counsels me; even at night my heart instructs me"* (Psalm 16:7). He remained open to receive counsel, instruction, correction, and direction, and maintained an open heart to commune with God 24/7.

* **David's heart was intentionally fixed on God.** *"I saw the Lord always before me. Because he is at my right hand, I will not be shaken"* (Acts 2:25). The word *intentional* is a word often used in the CHAYIL Glory Movement because our actions are specific, tactical,

and with an end in mind. David knew what he was doing, why he was doing it, and the predetermined outcome. When in meetings, he *set* the Lord before him. In times of trials, he *set* the Lord before him. When making decisions, he *set* the Lord before him. Whatever the news, the doctor, the lawyer, the people said, he *set* the Lord before him. He wrote, *"My heart, O God, is steadfast, my heart is steadfast; I will sing and make music. Awake, my soul! Awake, harp and lyre! I will awaken the dawn"* (Psalm 57:7-8). David intentionally controlled when his morning started to be with the lover of his soul.

* **David practiced obedience to God.** *"But from everlasting to everlasting the Lord's love is with those who fear him, and his righteousness with their children's children—with those who keep his covenant and remember to* **obey** *his precepts"* (Psalm 103:17-18 emphasis added). The paradox of David's life gives us hope and understanding of the strong nature of God's mercy. God testified concerning David, *"I have found David son of Jesse, a man after my own heart; he will do everything I want him to do"* (Acts 13:22). Interestingly, David's life was far from perfect and was a display of success and failure. God strategically recorded some of David's sins in the Bible, including his murder, lies, and adultery. Yet God boasted that David would do everything that He wanted him to do. It seems therefore that there is a difference between a heart that is bent on sin, fixed on sin, and determined to disobey God versus a heart that is fixed on God, steadfast and determined toward a godly lifestyle, but still has human imperfections. God knew that He could count on David to defend His cause; serve Him with His whole heart; worship Him in spirit and truth; when needed, risk his life to

please God and defend His kingdom; and sacrifice all to serve God. He knew that as long as David was alive, he had intimacy with a faithful son. David did not just give his tithes and offerings faithfully to God, but David's life was his main offering to God. David as a king maintained God as his priority and remained dependent on God as his source of glory.

* **David had great faith in God.** *"But I trust in your unfailing love; my heart rejoices in your salvation. I will sing to the Lord, for he has been good to me"* (Psalm 13:5-6). David declared this at his personal altar time when he was facing enemies and serious treachery. He knew that his enemies were predicting his fall and destruction. At times his own family failed him and joined in the slander of his enemies. But David's heart was fixed on the unfailing love of his King of glory, and he practiced immovable faith. While King Saul and his great soldiers were cowering in fear because of the giant Goliath, David, full of faith in God, decided to fight and conquer the giant. David's declaration to Goliath showed his heart of faith and his revelation on EL CHAYIL, Lord of armies, King of glory, Lord of wealth: *"David said to the Philistine, 'You come against me with sword and spear and javelin, but I come against you in the name of* **the Lord Almighty, the God of the armies of Israel***, whom you have defied'"* (1 Samuel 17:45 emphasis added). When our faith is in the Lord Almighty, all things are possible.

* **David knew how to access and receive glory from God.** David prayed, *"Summon your power, O God; show us your strength, O God, as you have done before"* (Psalm 68:28). David prayed like Moses, *"Show me your glory [strength, power, awesome majesty]"* (Exodus 33:18). David operated in the manifested glory

of EL CHAYIL. He was powerful, mighty, strong, wise, creative, and influential, with great favor and wealth, and with lasting eternal legacy. David was described as a man with *great glory*: *"Through the victories you gave, **his glory is great**; you have bestowed on him splendor and majesty. Surely you have granted him eternal blessings and made him glad with the joy of your presence"* (Psalm 21:5-6 emphasis added). David was made glad with the joy of the presence of God during his personal altar time. He had his meeting times with God, and he also nurtured continual communion with God.

* **David adored the law of God.** *"For I delight in your commands because I love them. I lift up my hands to your commands, which I love, and I meditate on your decrees"* (Psalm 119:47-48). Psalm 119, the longest Psalm in the Bible, with 176 verses, was written by David, and it was about his love for God's Word, His law, His precepts, and His commands. David expressed delight in meditating on God's Word. *To adore* means to hold something or someone with the utmost esteem, greatest love, and highest priority. David adored God and His Word. A personal altar includes worship, cleansing, Bible study, receiving instructions, and thanksgiving. God gave David His CHAYIL wisdom, understanding, insights, and revelation during his meditation on His Word. David had insights that were later revealed: *"In the beginning was the Word, and the Word was with God, and the Word was God"* (John 1:1). David, by meditating on God's Word at his personal altar, was actually meditating on God Himself and nurturing a heart after God. David's adoration of God's word was displayed: *"I seek you with all my heart; do not let me stray from your*

commands. I have hidden your word in my heart that I might not sin against you. Praise be to you, O Lord; teach me your decrees" (Psalm 119:10-12). By David adoring God's Word, He was actually adoring God.

* **David was truly repentant.** *"Have mercy on me, O God, according to your unfailing love; according to your great compassion blot out my transgressions. Wash away all my iniquity and cleanse me from my sin. For I know my transgressions, and my sin is always before me. Against you, you only, have I sinned and done what is evil in your sight, so that you are proved right when you speak and justified when you judge"* (Psalm 51:1-4). Here we see David crying out to God at his personal altar for mercy, forgiveness, cleansing, and deliverance. He had committed adultery and murder, and his true repentance was seen in this record of his personal altar. When confronted with his sin, he could have blamed Bathsheba, but he took all blame and in humility bore his soul before his King of glory, for in all of the consequences of his sin, his greatest fear was not the loss of his palace, his wealth, his health, or his life, but to lose the presence of His King of glory. He pleaded with God, *"Do not cast me from your presence or take your Holy Spirit from me. Restore to me the joy of your salvation and grant me a willing spirit, to sustain me"* (Psalm 51:11-12). True repentance is being sorry for our sins with a purpose that our love for God is greater than the desire for any sin and with a resolve to sin no more with God's help. David, in brilliance, negotiated with God that after his forgiveness, his testimony would bring God glory: *"Then I will teach transgressors your ways, and sinners will turn back to you"* (Psalm 51:13). David vowed to serve God by teaching others how to avoid sin and its consequences.

David demonstrated to us the power, privilege, passion, and pure joy at a personal altar. *"You have made known to me the path of life; you will fill me with joy in your presence, with eternal pleasures at your right hand"* (Psalm 16:11). He was a man after God's own heart, who prioritized being with God on a daily basis for sweet communion and fellowship with the Lover of his soul.

THE SECRET PLACE AT THE PERSONAL ALTAR

The Bible talks about a secret place in God and with God: *"You called in trouble, and I delivered you; I answered you **in the secret place** of thunder; I tested you at the waters of Meribah"* (Psalm 81:7 NKJV, emphasis added). There is a secret place where you can call on God in time of trouble. *"He who dwells in the secret place of the Most High Shall abide under the shadow of the Almighty. I will say of the Lord, 'He is my refuge and my fortress; My God, in Him I will trust'"* (Psalm 91:1 NKJV). There is a secret place where you can be hidden and be protected from the attacks of the enemy. Your secret place is your personal altar, exclusively yours for communion, intimacy, and fellowship in privacy with your King of glory. It is a secret place, a safe place, and a place of deliverance. In peaking into David's personal altar times for meeting with God, we can see his agenda that we can use as our model for successful quiet times with God. A personal altar includes: worship, Bible study and meditation, confession of sins, sharing hearts, receiving instructions, and thanksgiving.

THE AGENDA OF A PERSONAL ALTAR

1. ***Worship.*** Jesus tells us the protocol for entering into the secret place of God, our personal altar time with God: *"This, then, is how you should pray: 'Our Father in heaven, hallowed be your name'"* (Matthew 6:9). We begin with praise, worship, adoration, and exalting God for who He is and what He can do.

   This is very strategic because:

   a. **It first satisfies the desire of God who is seeking for worshipers.** *"Yet a time is coming and has now come when the true worshipers will worship the Father in spirit and truth, for they are the kind of worshipers the Father seeks. God is spirit, and his worshipers must worship in spirit and in truth"* (John 4:23-24). The word *seeks* involves passion. God is passionately seeking those whose heart is toward Him to make them strong and bless whatever they are doing (2 Chronicles 16:9). When we satisfy the desire of our King of glory, He will then satisfy ours.

   b. **It exalts God greater than our problems.** After worshiping God as your Lord Almighty, Lord of armies, King of glory, you could not believe that anything or anyone is greater than Him or that anything or any problem is too hard for Him to solve.

   c. **It puts you in your right mind.** God is not at the level of Satan, anyone, or anything. Jesus Christ is far above all and with a name that is greater than all. *"Which he exerted in Christ when he raised him from the dead and seated him at his right hand in the heavenly realms, far above all rule and authority, power and dominion, and* *every title that can be given, not only in the present age but also in the one to come. And God placed all things under his feet and appointed him to be head over everything for the church"* (Ephesians 1:20-22). In your right mind, you will not see Satan and his demons equal to God in power. Whatever problem you bring to God in your right mind, you will already have seen it defeated and bowing before the name of Jesus Christ.

    d. **It puts you in your right positioning.** *"And God raised us up with Christ and seated us with him in the heavenly realms in Christ Jesus"* (Ephesians 2:6). In your right positioning, you will not look up to demons and exalt them, but you will see them squirming under your feet in your positioning with Christ in the heavenly (spiritual) realms.

2. ***Bible study and meditation.*** As you read the Bible containing God's Word, also practice listening to His revelation, instruction, insights, correction, and tips on manifesting His glory. *"Open my eyes that I may see wonderful things in your law. I am a stranger on earth; do not hide your commands from me"* (Psalm 119:18-19). David did not read God's Word with a closed mind. He read, listened to, and meditated on the Word to discover nuggets of revelation. He asked God to open his spiritual eyes to see into the realm of the spirit. He lived in the realm of eternity and saw himself as a stranger on earth. This earth was not his eternal home. His decisions were in the light of eternity, the way he handled trials was in the light of eternity, and his sacrificial life was in the light of eternity. God's law, therefore, was important for Him to know God, to become like God on earth, and he did. *"After removing Saul, he made David their king. He testified*

concerning him: 'I have found David son of Jesse a man after my own heart; he will do everything I want him to do'" (Acts 13:22).

3. **Confession of sins.** David felt great relief after his time of confession before God. After his great failure that included adultery, lies, and murder, he was hiding from God. He feared so much the consequences of his sin after seeing how King Saul was dethroned by God for poorly handling his recurrent failures. He feared the greatest consequence of losing his great relationship with God. God sent a prophet to minister to David and to lead him into true repentance. David, after his repentance and restoration, rejoiced at his personal altar: *"Blessed is he whose transgressions are forgiven, whose sins are covered. Blessed is the man whose sin the Lord does not count against him and in whose spirit is no deceit"* (Psalm 32:1-2). Jesus died for the sins of the world. He invites us to come before Him and confess our sins because He knows about the gaps in our humanity and our weaknesses, tendencies, and imperfections. *"If we claim to be without sin, we deceive ourselves and the truth is not in us. If we confess our sins, he is faithful and just and will forgive us our sins and purify us from all unrighteousness. If we claim we have not sinned, we make him out to be a liar and his word has no place in our lives"* (1 John 1:8-10). God in His perfection provides for our imperfections and, by His precious blood, is always ready to forgive us, cleanse us, and restore us in the righteousness of Christ.

4. **Sharing hearts.** I have often wondered how David felt free to boldly go before God and ask Him to kill his enemies and sometimes even told God how to do it. I finally realized that in the beautiful loving and safe relationship between God and David, David felt safe in the

secret place of his personal altar to vent, be himself, share about his frustrations, and talk things through until he was in his right mind. Before His loving Savior, he felt he could expose fears, wavering faith, doubts, and discouragement because he experienced the great and secure love of God. This kind of freedom can be experienced in a healthy marriage, with trusted friends and with healthy parents. David shared openly with God. God did not love David because he was perfect but because David's heart was after Him.

In the secret place of his personal altar, David cried out to God, *"Arise, O Lord! Deliver me, O my God! Strike all my enemies on the jaw; break the teeth of the wicked"* (Psalm 3:7). Wow! That was intense, but David lived through some very intense times as a fugitive with a death sentence and bounty on his life. He could trust no one but God. He could cry before no one but God. After he vented before God, he ended with, *"From the Lord comes deliverance. May your blessing be on your people"* (Psalm 3:8). God's reaction to David's frustration was to hide and cover him in a safe place in His presence until he was restored and again in his right mind (with faith, courage, strength, and endurance). *"He will cover you with his feathers, and under his wings you will find refuge; his faithfulness will be your shield and rampart. You will not fear the terror of night, nor the arrow that flies by day"* (Psalm 91:4-5). Imagine God holding and rocking David as a baby crying in pain and singing to him softly until he felt safe again in his "mother's" (El Shaddai's) arms. David prayed, *"You are my hiding place; you will protect me from trouble and surround me with songs of deliverance"* (Psalm 32:7). A personal altar, God's secret place for you, is a place of unlimited love and compassion.

Not only did David share his heart, but God also shared His heart with His faithful servant and revealed the secrets of the Lord. *"The secret of the Lord is with those who fear Him, And He will show them His covenant"* (Psalm 25:14 NKJV). God has much to reveal to you in the secret place of your personal altar.

5. **Receiving instructions.** David was dependent on God as a shepherd looking after a few sheep and remained dependent as the King of Israel. He would enquire of the Lord what to do, when to do it, and how to do it. *"In the course of time, David inquired of the Lord. 'Shall I go up to one of the towns of Judah?' he asked. The Lord said, 'Go up.' David asked, 'Where shall I go?' 'To Hebron,' the Lord answered"* (2 Samuel 2:1). Here we see David asking what to do and where to go. David was in sync with God and knew the voice of His God.

Jesus shared how important this sharing time is to God: *"My sheep listen to my voice; I know them, and they follow me"* (John 10:27). As we practice meeting God at the personal altar, our spiritual hearing will be restored and we will hear and know His voice clearly. He will give instructions, and according to how we obey Him and follow His directions, our hearing will become even clearer. Listening (intentionally activating your spiritual ear to know His voice amidst your own thoughts) and obeying (acting upon what you heard) are proof that God's thoughts and instructions are of utmost importance to you. Your dependence on God is seen in the fruit of your life (your passion to meet with Him, to hear from Him, and to obey Him).

6. **Thanksgiving.** It is good to end our quiet time and personal altar with thanksgiving. As we study insights into David's communion time at his personal altar, we

see where he also placed emphasis on thanksgiving: *"I will praise God's name in song and glorify him with thanksgiving. This will please the Lord more than an ox, more than a bull with its horns and hoofs"* (Psalm 69:30-31). Thanksgiving pleases the Lord, so like David, it is good for us to develop and nurture a spirit of thanksgiving. To end our personal altar with thanksgiving will activate faith in God that He has heard and answered our prayers. *"Therefore I tell you, whatever you ask for in prayer, believe that you have received it, and it will be yours"* (Mark 11:24). Apostle Paul encourages us: *"Devote yourselves to prayer, being watchful and thankful"* (Colossians 4:2).

JESUS AND HIS PERSONAL ALTAR

Jesus was 100 percent man and 100 percent God, and yet He prioritized His communion time with His Heavenly Father at His personal altar. He lived a life that was dependent on His Father and the Holy Spirit. God became flesh as a man to teach us how to become like God in manifested (active) glory. The fruit of His prayer life at His personal altar was so powerful that the disciples asked Him to teach them how to pray effectively. Jesus went from His personal altar to making decisions, to growing in manifested glory, to preparing for the different seasons of His life, and to sharing the joy of His great communion and fellowship with His Father. He was Master of managing His time and priorities, what He did and with whom. His personal altar times were strategic, at different times, and at different places.

* ***His personal altar.*** He prayed on the mountainside alone: *"Immediately Jesus made the disciples get into the boat and go on ahead of him to the other side,*

A Personal Altar

while he dismissed the crowd. After he had dismissed them, he went up on a mountainside by himself to pray. When evening came, he was there alone" (Matthew 14:22-23). Jesus had a secret place near to the heart of His Father that was exclusively His alone, for worship, meditation, sharing hearts, receiving instructions, receiving fresh glory, and thanksgiving. Often there was a challenge with the demands of His family, ministry, and people but Jesus prioritized His personal altar as there is where He received glory to even follow through with the people's demands. The places where He had His personal altars were His refueling stations for the monumental call on His life.

* **Jesus prayed early in the morning.** Jesus prayed very early in the morning to avoid distractions, *"Very early in the morning, while it was still dark, Jesus got up, left the house and went off to a solitary place, where he prayed. Simon and his companions went to look for him, and when they found him, they exclaimed: 'Everyone is looking for you!'"* (Mark 1:35-37). Like David, He "awakened the dawn." In the early morning, there were no distractions, people were still asleep, there was no bustle of crowds and people moving around, and the markets were silent; it was as if He was the only person in the presence of His Father. Eventually as the people awoke, they began looking for Him, demanding His attention and even offended that He was not readily available. There was always a demand and battle for His time: *"Then Jesus' mother and brothers arrived. Standing outside, they sent someone in to call him. A crowd was sitting around him, and they told him, 'Your mother and brothers are outside looking for you'"* (Mark 3:31-32). However, Jesus remained Master of His time, priorities, and actions. He ruled His world in the

world. My book *The Ultimate Secret* states: "We are made in the image and likeness of God to speak like God words of faith to create and rule our world." We must be like Jesus to create and rule our world with prayer as the utmost priority. His personal altar time was non-negotiable: *"But Jesus often withdrew to lonely places and prayed"* (Luke 5:16).

* **Jesus prayed all night.** There were times when He sacrificed sleep for communion and direction from His Father: *"One of those days Jesus went out to a mountainside to pray, and spent the night praying to God. When morning came, he called his disciples to him and chose twelve of them, whom he also designated apostles"* (Luke 6:12-13). He wrestled with the kingdom of darkness continually as from His birth Satan tried to kill Him. He won the battle at His personal encounter with Satan by using the weapon of the Word of God: *"Jesus said to him, 'Away from me, Satan! For it is written: "Worship the Lord your God, and serve him only."' Then the devil left him, and angels came and attended him"* (Matthew 4:10-11).

* **Jesus prayed at His baptism.** Jesus prayed when He was being baptized in water, at His baptism in the Holy Spirit, and at the beginning of His public ministry. *"When all the people were being baptized, Jesus was baptized too. And as he was praying, heaven was opened and the Holy Spirit descended on him in bodily form like a dove. And a voice came from heaven: 'You are my Son, whom I love; with you I am well pleased'"* (Luke 3:21-22). This love exchange between Jesus and His Heavenly Father is a beautiful example of God's appreciation for our love for Him, which is seen in our obedience to Him, our dedication to His will on earth, and our communion even publicly with Him in open relationship.

* ***Jesus prayed before making critical decisions.*** Jesus communed with His Father for direction and instructions on choosing His disciples to help Him in His ministry: *"One of those days Jesus went out to a mountainside to pray, and spent the night praying to God. When morning came, he called his disciples to him and chose twelve of them, whom he also designated apostles"* (Luke 6:12-13). From the place of His personal altar where He communed with His Father all night, He was able to choose His disciples from among those who were following Him. Jesus depended on His Father when making critical decisions.

* ***Jesus prayed after ministry and miracles.*** *"The number of those who ate was about five thousand men, besides women and children. Immediately Jesus made the disciples get into the boat and go on ahead of him to the other side, while he dismissed the crowd. After he had dismissed them, he went up on a mountainside by himself to pray. When evening came, he was there alone, but the boat was already a considerable distance from land, buffeted by the waves because the wind was against it"* (Matthew 14:21-24). Jesus prayed before and after ministry. He prayed before to receive glory, and He prayed after with thanksgiving, for refueling and to rest and be restored in His Father's grace.

* ***Jesus prayed before releasing critical information.*** Jesus knew the time to confirm with His disciples that He was God. *"Once when Jesus was praying in private and his disciples were with him, he asked them, 'Who do the crowds say I am?' They replied, 'Some say John the Baptist; others say Elijah; and still others, that one of the prophets of long ago has come back to life.' 'But what about you?' he asked. 'Who do you say I am?' Peter answered,*

'The Christ of God'" (Luke 9:18-20). Timing is critical in the journey of life.

* **Jesus isolated Himself in prayer for protection.** "Jesus, knowing that they intended to come and make him king by force, withdrew again to a mountain by himself" (John 6:15). He protected Himself from the zeal and accolades of people because He knew their fickleness, which was either based on ignorance or selfish ambition. The prophets and kings suffered at the hands of zealous although well-meaning people. His times and promotion were in the hands of His Father. Man could not make Him King by force. He was EL CHAYIL, Lord of armies, King of glory, Lord of Wealth.

* **Jesus ruled His world with prayer.** Jesus was not distracted by His fame. He knew that the same people who cried "Hosanna" would in a few days also cry, "Crucify Him." He knew that the same people He healed would try to wound Him. People demanded His time, but He was not a people-pleaser because His dependence was on His Father and the Holy Spirit. *"Yet the news about him spread all the more, so that crowds of people came to hear him and to be healed of their sicknesses. But Jesus often withdrew to lonely places and prayed"* (Luke 5:15-16). He was not controlled by the needs of the people—the poor, the sick, the demonized, and the needy. When criticized, He replied, *"You will always have the poor among you, but you will not always have me"* (John 12:8). He knew that if he healed a thousand sick people, there would be thousands still in need. Jesus loved the poor, He loved the people, but He controlled His time with the right priorities according to the will of His Father.

* ***Jesus prayed in times of temptation and crisis.*** *"Then Jesus went with his disciples to a place called Gethsemane, and he said to them, 'Sit here while I go over there and pray'"* (Matthew 26:36). *"Jesus went out as usual to the Mount of Olives, and his disciples followed him. On reaching the place, he said to them, 'Pray that you will not fall into temptation.' He withdrew about a stone's throw beyond them, knelt down and prayed, 'Father, if you are willing, take this cup from me; yet not my will, but yours be done.' An angel from heaven appeared to him and strengthened him. And being in anguish, he prayed more earnestly, and his sweat was like drops of blood falling to the ground"* (Luke 22:39-44). Jesus agonized in Gethsemane at the thought of the cruel suffering, shame, and vile sins that He would need to take on at the cross. He freely shared His heart and concerns at His personal altar, that secret, safe, and secure place. His Father comforted Him, gave Him instructions, and sent an angel to strengthen Him. There is unlimited power at the personal altar.

* ***Jesus prayed during His final hours on the cross.*** *"Jesus said, 'Father, forgive them, for they do not know what they are doing.' And they divided up his clothes by casting lots"* (Luke 23:34). Jesus had a personal altar on the cross, and He remained in communion and connected with His Father and His Holy Spirit for the release of glory for Him to endure the cross. He took the lashes; He allowed them to nail His hands and feet to the cross, curse and mock Him, pierce His side, give Him bitter vinegar to drink when He was thirsty, and shame Him ruthlessly. When it was finished and His kingdom-legal transaction was satisfied with punishment, shame, and curses, He cried out, *"It is finished"*

(John 19:30). His last words to His Father He cried out triumphantly: *"Jesus called out with a loud voice, 'Father, into your hands I commit my spirit.' When he had said this, he breathed his last"* (Luke 23:46). His final words were directed in prayer to His Father, and His final action before He died was personal prayer to His Father. Jesus died in prayer.

Our awesome Savior, Jesus Christ, and our great heroes of the Bible such as Abraham, Isaac, Jacob, Moses, Daniel, David, kings, prophets, Mary, disciples, apostles, and ministers showed in their lives the importance of their personal altars. Abraham's encounters with God at his personal altar made him great as the father of the Hebrew religion and in the genealogy of Jesus; Daniel confronted evil principalities and delivered Israel at his personal altar; Moses delivered and ruled millions of Israelites from instructions at his personal altar; and the apostles birthed and established Christianity from the glory and instructions they received at their personal altars. There is power at a personal altar.

CHAPTER 4

A Family Altar

So Jacob said to his household and to all who were with him...Then come, let us go up to Bethel, where I will build an altar to God (Genesis 35:2,3).

In the beginning, God created a man and He named him Adam. God had a personal relationship with Adam, and they would meet regularly for communion and fellowship. Adam was responsible to create and develop the earth as a co-laborer with God, a family project. Eventually God established the family: *"The Lord God said, 'It is not good for the man to be alone. I will make a helper suitable for him'"* (Genesis 2:18). The Lord then made a woman, and she was called Eve. God performed the first marriage and blessed Adam and Eve as husband and wife to reproduce, create a family, and develop the world as God's kingdom on earth. The process of reproduction and growth of human families would continue until the earth was populated with a people that God would call His earthly family. God created families and has a heart for families. The family is the unit of society, and children are the future of our world.

The *family altar* is therefore very important to God as it is a time of communion, consecration, and dedication of the family. God is our Heavenly Father, and He wants to have family time with His earthly family. *"For this reason I kneel before the Father, from whom his whole family in heaven and on earth derives its name"* (Ephesians 3:14-15). Jesus told us to call God, "Father." It is a great privilege to be of the family of God, with the Almighty God in such great relationship with us, with His desire to Father us, protect us, provide for us, and prepare us as His glorified representatives on earth. We were made in the spiritual DNA of God our Father, in His image and likeness, to reflect Him, represent Him, and reproduce for Him on earth. *"So God created man in His own image; in the image of God He created him; male and female He created them. Then God blessed them, and God said to them, 'Be fruitful and multiply; fill the earth and subdue it; have dominion over the fish of the sea, over the birds of the air, and over every living thing that moves on the earth'"* (Genesis 1:27-28 NKJV). We were created to participate in a great family project—the development of God's kingdom on earth.

As the family of God, we are powerful, with great privilege, but we can only accomplish all that we are supposed to do with the help of God. The family altar is therefore very important so that families and children can grow in intimacy with God and fulfill their purpose in God. After Abraham received his calling to establish a family of God that would be set apart from a world characterized by paganism and rejection of God, the first thing he did was to build an altar for communion, consecration, and fellowship with God. *"The Lord appeared to Abram and said, 'To your offspring I will give this land.' So he built an altar there to the Lord, who had appeared to him"* (Genesis 12:7). Notice that God's covenant with Abraham was not only for him, his wife Sarah, and his immediate family, but it included offspring for generations.

ABRAHAM'S FAMILY ALTAR

The family altar was very important to Abraham, and everywhere the family relocated, Abraham built a family altar. *"From there he went on toward the hills east of Bethel and pitched his tent, with Bethel on the west and Ai on the east. There he built an altar to the Lord and called on the name of the Lord"*

A Family Altar

(Genesis 12:8). Abraham made it known to God and his family that he respected his covenant with God, was dependent on God, honored God, and that his family was dedicated unto God.

The family altar is a place for family worship, Bible study and meditation, confession of sins, sharing hearts, receiving instructions, and thanksgiving. It is a time for strengthening relationship with God and relationships in the family. Abraham practiced and passed down the family altar that today is still practiced and maintained among Jews and Christians. The family altar, therefore, is important to pass down godly principles to children and generations forever.

> Hear, O Israel: The Lord our God, the Lord is one. Love the Lord your God with all your heart and with all your soul and with all your strength. These commandments that I give you today are to be upon your hearts. Impress them on your children. Talk about them when you sit at home and when you walk along the road, when you lie down and when you get up. Tie them as symbols on your hands and bind them on your foreheads. Write them on the doorframes of your houses and on your gates (Deuteronomy 6:4-9).

For Abraham, the family altar was not just for a tradition, but to preserve relationship with God for intimacy, service, and lasting legacy. Abraham's children participated in the family altar as a prioritized family practice, and the practice continued for generations in their children's children. God must remain the Father, King, and Savior of the family.

Isaac built a family altar and established relationship with the God of his father Abraham.

> From there he went up to Beersheba. That night the Lord appeared to him and said, "I am the God of your father Abraham. Do not be afraid, for I am with you; I will bless you and will increase the number of your descendants for the sake of my servant Abraham." Isaac built an altar there and called on the name of the

Lord. There he pitched his tent, and there his servants dug a well (Genesis 26:23-25).

Isaac built a family altar at his home and called on the name of the Lord just as his father, Abraham, did. The relationship between Abraham and God was so great that God named Himself the God of Abraham. The relationship between Isaac also was strong, and he activated the covenant with God and his father, so God renamed Himself the God of Abraham and Isaac.

Jacob built a family altar and established relationship with the God of his fathers, Abraham and Isaac.

After Jacob came from Paddan Aram, he arrived safely at the city of Shechem in Canaan and camped within sight of the city. For a hundred pieces of silver, he bought from the sons of Hamor, the father of Shechem, the plot of ground where he pitched his tent. There he set up an altar and called it El Elohe Israel (Genesis 33:18-20).

Jacob prayed to activate the covenant blessing of his grandfather Abraham and father Isaac: *"Then Jacob prayed, 'O God of my father Abraham, God of my father Isaac, O Lord, who said to me, "Go back to your country and your relatives, and I will make you prosper"'"* (Genesis 32:9). After Jacob made his vows to God and a decision to serve God and to rely on God as His Heavenly Father, God was named the God of Abraham, Isaac, and Jacob: *"Then he said, 'I am the God of your father, the God of Abraham, the God of Isaac and the God of Jacob.' At this, Moses hid his face, because he was afraid to look at God"* (Exodus 3:6). Notice that God called Himself the God of Abraham, the God of Isaac, and the God of Jacob and now would embrace Moses in a covenant relationship for CHAYIL glory to flow in and through him as deliverer of the Israelites who were in slavery.

The family altar strengthens relationship with parents and children for the generational legacy of being a part of the family of God eternally, which is the heart of God our Father. God's covenant with Abraham, Isaac, and Jacob is so strong and eternal that the covenant blessing and protection can be activated in each generation that calls on God. Hundreds of years later, the descendants of Abraham were being tormented by the King of Egypt, and God remembered the covenant of protection that He made with Abraham, Isaac, and Jacob: *"God heard their groaning and he remembered his covenant with Abraham, with Isaac and with Jacob. So God looked on the Israelites and was concerned about them"* (Exodus 2:23-25). Now you can activate this covenant of blessing, protection, and provision through faith in Jesus Christ, son of Abraham and son of David. *"He [Christ] redeemed us in order that the blessing given to Abraham might come to the Gentiles through Christ Jesus, so that by faith we might receive the promise of the Spirit"* (Galatians 3:14).

JACOB RESTORED HIS FAMILY ALTAR

Jacob had to restore the family altar that was broken down.

> Then God said to Jacob, "Go up to Bethel and settle there, and build an altar there to God, who appeared to you when you were fleeing from your brother Esau." So Jacob said to his household and to all who were with him, "Get rid of the foreign gods you have with you, and purify yourselves and change your clothes. Then come, let us go up to Bethel, where I will build an altar to God, who answered me in the day of my distress and who has been with me wherever I have gone." So they gave Jacob all the foreign gods they had and the rings in their ears, and Jacob buried them under the oak at Shechem (Genesis 35:1-5).

When the family altar is disregarded, it is easy for the world's culture and acts of pagan worship to infuse a family with dangerous consequences. God appeared to Jacob to shape up with his family priority and take back dominion in his home, with Jehovah God as the God of his household. Satan looks for opportunities to entice people to minimize their relationship with God.

THE AGENDA OF A FAMILY ALTAR

The agenda of a family altar is similar to that of a personal and other altars, as the protocol and purpose of prayer in all formats are similar.

1. **Worship.** A family altar is to affirm that Christ is the Head of your home and therefore worship, prayer and acknowledging Him is very important. Joshua was a determined leader of Israel and his household: *"But if serving the Lord seems undesirable to you, then choose for yourselves this day whom you will serve, whether the gods your forefathers served beyond the River, or the gods of the Amorites, in whose land you are living.* **But as for me and my household, we will serve the Lord**" (Joshua 24:15 emphasis added). God was worshiped in his heart and life, and His worship was a priority in his home. At a family altar, God becomes the Father of a father, a mother, and children in intimate and acknowledged relationship. God's role of Father in the home creates faith and expectation of His provision, protection, and care. As Heavenly Father, He is worshiped honored and revered. Gratefulness to Jesus Christ, our Savior, King of glory, is given and thankfulness for our Holy

Spirit, helper and strength is expressed. When God is worshiped by a family, the family is in His secret place for lasting legacy.

2. ***Bible study and meditation.*** When a family reads the Bible together, respect for His Word, reverence for His Word will become a reality that result in obedience to His Word. In a family, values should be based on God's Word and not what is popular in society or taught in schools. The anti-Christ spirit has infused all societies bringing confusion and deception. The Word of God is being twisted with lies and deception and many are being subdued in a tolerant society to accept the lies of Satan. This happened with Adam and Eve and they lost their glory and great relationship with God, their Father. The home has to be a place of teaching and reinforcing God's Word, principles, and values. A family altar is powerful to protect families and prevent further destruction of societies and our world.

3. ***Confession of sins.*** Confessions and sharing weaknesses can be a meaningful time in families where the spirit of humility is demonstrated by parents and children. *"Therefore confess your sins to each other and pray for each other so that you may be healed. The prayer of a righteous man is powerful and effective"* (James 5:16). Sins are imperfections, "missing the mark of perfection." We are therefore all sinners and need a place to share weaknesses, shortcomings, and failures in a safe place of help, accountability, restoration, and encouragement.

4. ***Sharing hearts.*** In CHAYIL Power Groups, the time of interactive sharing is very strategic and powerful and can be practiced at altars in family or groups.

Facilitating CHAYIL Power Groups, family altars, or prayer groups includes:

* ***Welcome, prayer, worship***
* ***One-word check in.*** Use one word to describe how you are feeling today. Be real so that others can celebrate you and your testimony, or if you have an issue, you can receive prayer or collective wisdom (ideas and experiences) from other members.
* ***One-word explanation.*** Explain your "one-word" check in for celebration, prayer, or peer coaching (if you so desire).
* ***Peer coaching.*** Peer coaching is when a member of the group shares an issue for which they would like to receive ideas, wisdom, and strategies from the experiences of other members in the group. Everyone will get opportunities to share or receive coaching from others.
* ***Interactive discussion*** of CHAYIL Daily Inspiration.
* ***Training in CHAYIL pillars: Worship, Wisdom, Power, Honor, Favor, Wealth, Influence.*** Choose a pillar for discussion. How will you intentionally grow in that pillar? Share at next session for accountability.
* ***One-word check out.*** How are you feeling? Members share how they are feeling after being in the CHAYIL Power Group.
* ***Evangelism and growth.***
* ***Prayer and intercession.*** At the end of the group time, an altar of intercession with the power of agreement is created to pray for the needs of members, family, ministry, business, etc. Altar of intercession—Exodus 17:10-13; power of agreement—Matthew 18:18-20.

* ***Love and fellowship.*** In the interactive times of sharing and caring, helping family bonds and relationships are strengthened. Peer coaching is powerful as each member of the family or group contributes to an issue. Strengths and gifts of each member are discovered, validated, and celebrated.
5. ***Receiving instructions.*** Family members are trained to hear from God and get to know His voice. Training in hearing the voice of God can be very stimulating and motivating. It deepens the relationship with God and activates prophetic revelations.
6. ***Thanksgiving.*** In a culture of honor and gratefulness, hearts of thanksgiving and the expression of thanksgiving are cultivated. It is good to end our quiet time and personal altar with thanksgiving to God and to be thankful for each member of the family. *"Be joyful always; pray continually; give thanks in all circumstances, for this is God's will for you in Christ Jesus"* (1 Thessalonians 5:16-18).

A family altar is built with unmovable pillars of conviction (it is important), commitment (it is a priority), covenant (relationship with God and each other as the family of God), and sacrifice (time, energy). There are many excuses for not having a family altar, family devotions, and family prayer time. Everyone is too busy. This is obviously a battle because the family altar creates an atmosphere of blessing and protection in the home and strengthens relationships.

It helps when we realize that the family altar is:

* ***A command.*** *"Be careful, or you will be enticed to turn away and worship other gods and bow down to them. Then the Lord's anger will burn against you, and he will shut the heavens so that it will not rain and the ground will yield no produce,*

and you will soon perish from the good land the Lord is giving you. Fix these words of mine in your hearts and minds; tie them as symbols on your hands and bind them on your foreheads. Teach them to your children, talking about them when you sit at home and when you walk along the road, when you lie down and when you get up. Write them on the doorframes of your houses and on your gates, so that your days and the days of your children may be many in the land that the Lord swore to give your forefathers, as many as the days that the heavens are above the earth"* (Deuteronomy 11:16-21).

* **A privilege.** *"The children of your servants will live in your presence; their descendants will be established before you"* (Psalm 102:28).

* **A joy.** *"You have made known to me the path of life; you will fill me with joy in your presence, with eternal pleasures at your right hand"* (Psalm 16:11).

CHAPTER 5

A Home Altar

They replied, "Believe in the Lord Jesus, and you will be saved—you and your household" (Acts 16:31).

A *home altar* is intentionally built to establish the owner and head of the home as Jesus Christ for His habitation. *"Do not defile the land where you live and where I dwell, for I, the Lord, dwell among the Israelites"* (Numbers 35:34). With this in mind, the actions in our homes intentionally recognize our Lord as Owner. Even as He takes permanent residence in our hearts as His home, He dwells among us in our homes. *"Here I am! I stand at the door and knock. If anyone hears my voice and opens the door, I will come in and eat with him, and he with me"* (Revelation 3:20). A *family altar* is the gathering of a family for devotions, prayer, and time of sharing. A family altar can be at any location and not necessarily at your home. When a family is on vacation, the family altar can be in a hotel, on a beach, at a park, or at any location. God is omnipresent—He is everywhere all at once. He lives in heaven, seated on a throne, and at the same time He is in hearts, homes, and communities where He is invited to bring His kingdom and angels.

Once Jesus Christ is welcomed as the Head of your home, as His dwelling place, your home is never empty. *"My dwelling place will be with them; I will be their God, and they will be my people"* (Ezekiel 37:27). The Lord and His angels claim the land and home as property of His kingdom. Your home becomes a secret place of the Most High. *"He who dwells in the secret place of the Most High shall abide under the shadow of the Almighty. I will say of the Lord, 'He is my refuge and my fortress; My God, in Him I will trust'"* (Psalm 91:1-2 NKJV). Your home is blessed and is a blessing to all who live in your home.

In a study of the home of Obed-Edom, we see where the presence of the ark (altar) of the Lord in his home resulted in the blessing of his home, family, and everything he had.

> The ark [altar] of the Lord remained in the house of Obed-Edom the Gittite for three months, and the Lord blessed him and his entire household. Now King David was told, "The Lord has blessed the household of Obed-Edom and everything he has, **because of the ark of God**." So David went down and brought up the ark of God from the house of Obed-Edom to the City of David with rejoicing. When those who were carrying the ark of the Lord had taken six steps, he sacrificed a bull and a fattened calf. David, wearing a linen ephod, danced before the Lord with all his might, while he and the entire house of Israel brought up the ark of the Lord with shouts and the sound of trumpets (2 Samuel 6:11-15 emphasis added).

An altar to our King of glory is powerful because it is intentionally created to invite His presence and power for manifested glory (blessings).

The ark of the Lord was the most important piece of furniture in the tabernacle and temple. It was the centerpiece in the tabernacle in the Holy of Holies where God's holy presence resided. The presence of God in the Holy of Holies in the tabernacle was so powerful that only the high priest was allowed to enter, and only if he was clean or he would immediately die. *"The Lord said to Moses: 'Tell your brother Aaron not to come whenever he chooses into the Most Holy Place behind the curtain in front of the atonement cover on the ark,*

A Home Altar

or else he will die, because I appear in the cloud over the atonement cover'" (Leviticus 16:2). The presence and power of our Lord Almighty was awesome and was to be respected, pointing to the time when He would live in the hearts of His believing Christians.

The powerful presence of the Lord in the ark killed one of David's men who violated the principle of handling, carrying, transporting, and respecting God's powerful presence in the ark. David was angry and scared of touching the ark:

> David was afraid of the Lord that day and said, "How can the ark of the Lord ever come to me?" He was not willing to take the ark of the Lord to be with him in the City of David. Instead, he took it aside to the house of Obed-Edom the Gittite. The ark of the Lord remained in the house of Obed-Edom the Gittite for three months, and the Lord blessed him and his entire household (2 Samuel 6:9-11).

Obed-Edom volunteered to have the ark of the Lord at his house, and God blessed him and his entire household (family, business, and relationships). When a home altar is established by faith in a home, it becomes a *blessed home*. When David finally restored the ark to Israel, it became a *blessed land*. When the ark was in the temple, it was blessed and the people worshiping in the temple were blessed. Wherever the presence of the Lord God abides (in a heart, home, church, school, workplace, community, or nation), by special invitation it is blessed.

God will set up His kingdom wherever He is invited:

* **In our hearts.** *"We know that we live in him and he in us, because he has given us of his Spirit"* (1 John 4:13). *"I have been crucified with Christ and I no longer live, but Christ lives in me. The life I live in the body, I live by faith in the Son of God, who loved me and gave himself for me"* (Galatians 2:20).

* ***In our homes.*** *"Now King David was told, 'The Lord has blessed the household of Obed-Edom and everything he has, because of the ark of God.' So David went down and brought up the ark of God from the house of Obed-Edom to the City of David with rejoicing"* (2 Samuel 6:12).
* ***In His Church.*** *"One thing I ask of the Lord, this is what I seek: that I may dwell in the house of the Lord all the days of my life, to gaze upon the beauty of the Lord and to seek him in his temple"* (Psalm 27:4).
* ***Among a community.*** *"And I will live among the Israelites and will not abandon my people Israel"* (1 Kings 6:13).

God is waiting for invitations. *"Here I am! I stand at the door and knock. If anyone hears my voice and opens the door, I will come in and eat with him, and he with me"* (Revelation 3:19-20).

A home altar is built like all altars to our King of glory. It is:

1. ***Spiritual not physical.*** We do not build a physical place or set up idols, candles, pictures of the dead, or any man-made furniture or symbol. *"But the rest of mankind, who were not killed by these plagues, did not repent of the works of their hands, that they should not worship demons, and idols of gold, silver, brass, stone, and wood, which can neither see nor hear nor walk"* (Revelation 9:20 NKJV). God is Spirit and is omnipresent. Altars are spiritual not physical. Under the Old Covenant, the ark and altars were physical and symbolic, as were the sacrifices of animals, grain offerings, burnt offerings, and other rituals. Those were shadows leading up to the time when God became a man called Jesus who fulfilled the law and satisfied fully the rights for God to dwell in us and we in Him. We now have

direct access to God 24/7. Our worship to God is spiritual: *"Yet a time is coming and has now come when the true worshipers will worship the Father in spirit and truth, for they are the kind of worshipers the Father seeks. God is spirit, and his worshipers must worship in spirit and in truth"* (John 4:23-24).

2. ***Built intentionally.*** We intentionally invite Jesus into our home so that our property and home is claimed and given back to His kingdom. *"Here I am! I stand at the door and knock. If anyone hears my voice and opens the door, I will come in and eat with him, and he with me"* (Revelation 3:19-20). We ask God to fill our home with His Holy angels, we renounce Satan and his demons, and we declare our home as a no-flight zone for demons and evil spirits.

3. ***Built with expectations.*** *"The ark of the Lord remained in the house of Obed-Edom the Gittite for three months, and the Lord blessed him and his entire household"* (2 Samuel 6:11). By faith we expect our home to be blessed, our family to be blessed, our household to be blessed as we give ownership to everything that we own to God, and everyone who comes into our home will be blessed. Our home is a meeting place with God and a place of hospitality and blessing to others.

4. ***Built as a home of prayer and intercession.*** *"I tell you the truth, whatever you bind on earth will be bound in heaven, and whatever you loose on earth will be loosed in heaven. Again, I tell you that if two of you on earth agree about anything you ask for, it will be done for you by my Father in heaven. For where two or three come together in my name, there am I with them"* (Matthew 18:18-20).

5. ***Built for kingdom revelation and government.*** At a home altar, the ownership, government, and kingdom of God is established, with Jesus as our King of glory. The power of His presence in our hearts, homes, community, and nation subdues evil influences and establishes His kingdom. We provide a legal ground for His kingdom to be established for **Mission INFUSION,** which is, "To infuse the CHAYIL glory of the Lord Jesus Christ in every heart, home, community, and nation." The angels' declaration shall be a reality: *"And they were calling to one another: 'Holy, holy, holy is the Lord Almighty; the whole earth is full of his glory'"* (Isaiah 6:3).

6. ***Built by faith declaration.*** *"You will also declare a thing, And it will be established for you; So light will shine on your ways"* (Job 22:28 NKJV). We know what we are doing, we say what we are doing, and we expect results. *"Now faith is the substance of things hoped for, the evidence of things not seen"* (Hebrews 11:1 NKJV).

A home altar to our King of glory marks a home with the blood of Jesus Christ, the presence of His holy angels, and a territory claimed by the kingdom of God. Your home that was previously in the kingdom of the enemy is now reclaimed and back in the kingdom of God. *"So I have come down to rescue them from the hand of the Egyptians and to bring them up out of that land into a good and spacious land, a land flowing with milk and honey—the home of the Canaanites, Hittites, Amorites, Perizzites, Hivites and Jebusites"* (Exodus 3:7-8). Home and land ownership by God's people is very important to God, as ownership of land and resources makes a kingdom powerful and influential. Through Joseph, the king of Egypt became powerful, influential, and wealthy because of the land acquisition campaign that Joseph created. Joseph established

Israel with their own land in Egypt: *"So Joseph settled his father and his brothers in Egypt and gave them property in the best part of the land, the district of Rameses, as Pharaoh directed"* (Genesis 47:11). Then Joseph seized the opportunity to trade food in a time of famine for land: *"So Joseph bought all the land in Egypt for Pharaoh. The Egyptians, one and all, sold their fields, because the famine was too severe for them. The land became Pharaoh's"* (Genesis 47:20).

God has specific homes for His family:

> From one man he made every nation of men, that they should inhabit the whole earth; and he determined the times set for them and **the exact places where they should live**. God did this so that men would seek him and perhaps reach out for him and find him, though he is not far from each one of us. "For in him we live and move and have our being." As some of your own poets have said, "We are his offspring" (Acts 17:26-28 emphasis added).

Where you live, God lives. Where you are, God is.

It is harvest time. Now is the day of salvation. Now is the season of restoration. *"For he says, 'In the time of my favor I heard you, and in the day of salvation I helped you'"* (2 Corinthians 6:2). God loves the world and will save our world. *"For God so loved the world that he gave his one and only Son, that whoever believes in him shall not perish but have eternal life. For God did not send his Son into the world to condemn the world, but to save the world through him"* (John 3:16-17). God owns the earth and will save the people, His land, and His resources (wealth, gifts, talents, glory). *"The earth is the Lord's, and everything in it, the world, and all who live in it"* (Psalm 24:1). God is looking for hearts and homes to claim as His own so that His presence and power can freely bless, save, protect, and provide. God wants a family of families. *"For this reason I kneel before the Father, from whom his whole family in heaven and on earth derives its name"* (Ephesians 3:14-15). Your heart is His home, and your home is His.

CHAPTER 6

A Community Altar

So Gideon built an altar to the Lord there and called it The Lord is Peace. To this day it stands in Ophrah of the Abiezrites (Judges 6:24).

A *community altar* to our King of glory, the Lord Jesus Christ, is built by faith in a school, workplace, or any facility where you have the authority, with the intention to invite Jesus Christ to come and establish His kingdom at that place. God has given a promise that states His intention: *"Then the seventh angel sounded: And there were loud voices in heaven, saying, 'The kingdoms of this world have become the kingdoms of our Lord and of His Christ, and He shall reign forever and ever!'"* (Revelation 11:15 NKJV). God will appoint strategic experienced CHAYIL servants to positions of influence in all the kingdoms of this world. *"The decision is announced by messengers, the holy ones declare the verdict, so that the living may know that the Most High is sovereign over the kingdoms of men and gives them to anyone he wishes and sets over them the lowliest of men"* (Daniel 4:17). God's kingdom will infuse the kingdoms of this world with His glory. He will display His glory among the nations (Ezekiel 39:21).

The kingdom of God is the reign of God in heaven and on earth in lives, societies, and territories. Wherever God is invited to bring His kingdom, He comes. Wherever a door is opened for God to come in with His presence, He comes. Wherever you go, the kingdom of God is present and near to others, waiting for an invitation. *"From that time on Jesus began to preach,*

'Repent, for the kingdom of heaven is near'" (Matthew 4:17). God's plan is to open doors for you to bring His kingdom that is *in* you to be established *by* you in that place or organization. **CHAYIL glory** is the manifested power and glory of our Lord Jesus Christ *in* and *through* His servants. **Mission INFUSION** is to infuse the CHAYIL glory of the Lord Jesus Christ in every heart, home, community, and nation.

Jesus has given us His command and authority to disciple nations.

> Then Jesus came to them and said, "All authority in heaven and on earth has been given to me. Therefore go and make disciples of all nations, baptizing them in the name of the Father and of the Son and of the Holy Spirit, and teaching them to obey everything I have commanded you. And surely I am with you always, to the very end of the age" (Matthew 28:18-20).

The word *authority* means the right to rule, the right to have influence, or the right to display glory. We go and disciple nations by influencing one person, one home, one facility, or one community at a time.

When you are given authority by God to infuse our world with His glory, all Heaven is behind you with their support, protection, and provision. You are God's ambassador, a CHAYIL agent in His Majesty's service, to represent His kingdom in a particular place and territory on earth. The door your King opens for you no one can close. You no longer just go to a school, but you see yourself as God's CHAYIL agent in His Majesty's service. You are no longer just hired in a job, but positioned there as God's CHAYIL agent in His Majesty's service. When you are not just hired, you cannot just be fired because the kingdom of God rules the kingdoms of this world. As God's CHAYIL agent in His Majesty's service, your ethics, values, and behavior represent His kingdom and bring glory to Him by who you are, what you say, and what you do. God,

A Community Altar

however, will move you from place to place when He is ready for you to have influence in another workplace, school, or territory. You don't just own a business or a company, but you have been given dominion, power, and glory to rule over products, services, staff, and wealth in God's kingdom. *"Then the sovereignty, power and greatness of the kingdoms under the whole heaven will be handed over to the saints, the people of the Most High. His kingdom will be an everlasting kingdom, and all rulers will worship and obey him"* (Daniel 7:27).

Ambassadors of Christ will be positioned in places of influence to build community altars to our King of glory so that His kingdom of righteousness (salvation and values), peace (health, well-being, and prosperity), and joy (Jesus Christ exalted in worship in unity of purpose) can influence our world until the whole earth is filled with His glory. *"We are therefore Christ's ambassadors, as though God were making his appeal through us. We implore you on Christ's behalf: Be reconciled to God"* (2 Corinthians 5:20). An ambassador in an official representative of a kingdom, a government, or an organization. In kingdoms and governments, an ambassador is a high-ranking diplomat with power, privileges, and a strategic purpose.

Government Ambassador	God's Kingdom Ambassador
Represents a government and country	Represents the kingdom of God
Stationed in a foreign capital	Stationed on earth
Allowed control of an embassy	Allowed control of a school or workplace
Given diplomatic immunity and power	Given diplomatic immunity and power
Protects citizens of his home country in his host country	Protects Christian citizens

Government Ambassador	God's Kingdom Ambassador
Supports opportunities to prosper their country	Support opportunities to prosper the kingdom of God
Works for peace	Works to establish peace in hearts and communities
Works against corruption	Works against demonic forces of evil and corruption
Works to advance the agenda of his country	Works to advance the agenda of the kingdom of God to fill the earth with the glory of our Lord Jesus Christ

When you build an altar to our King of glory, the Lord Jesus Christ, in your community and make a declaration for His presence and kingdom to come and be established in that place, He comes in His power for manifested glory. *"Your kingdom come, your will be done on earth as it is in heaven"* (Matthew 6:10). By faith, His presence is established in hearts, communities, and nations for His mercy, peace, and power to transform lives and communities. His kingdom (government and purpose) will come and rule in that place.

When Abraham started his journey of faith in God, he moved from his family home and country to find his new settlement. His nephew Lot went with him, and they worked together for many years, building their business and families. After a while, however, Abraham and Lot had to part ways because of continual differences in interests that led to feuds. Abraham decided to make a peaceful separation and let Lot choose his portion of land and settlement. Abraham built a community altar to God to mark his land and family for God's continued blessing, protection, and provision.

God coached Abram how to mark his land, claim it, and confirm it as a generational legacy in the kingdom of God.

A Community Altar

The Lord said to Abram after Lot had parted from him, "Lift up your eyes from where you are and look north and south, east and west. All the land that you see I will give to you and your offspring forever. I will make your offspring like the dust of the earth, so that if anyone could count the dust, then your offspring could be counted. Go, walk through the length and breadth of the land, for I am giving it to you." So Abram moved his tents and went to live near the great trees of Mamre at Hebron, where he built an altar to the Lord (Genesis 13:14-18).

Here we see the following principles for establishing God's kingdom in a community: 1. See it and pray it. 2. Walk it and claim it. 3. Dream it and design it. 4. Occupy it and rule it. 5. Establish the kingdom of God by building an altar to the Lord. *"Here I am! I stand at the door and knock. If anyone hears my voice and opens the door, I will come in and eat with him, and he with me"* (Revelation 3:20). The kingdom of God comes near a community through you, to be established in that community for occupation, blessing, government, and peace.

When you build a community altar to the King of glory in your business or organization, the blessings of the kingdom of God will be upon all that you commit unto Him. *"'Does Job fear God for nothing?' Satan replied. 'Have you not put a hedge around him and his household and everything he has? You have blessed the work of his hands, so that his flocks and herds are spread throughout the land'"* (Job 1:9-10). Job was a powerful man with a great business, a large family, and a large staff. He was not only a businessman, but he was also the priest of his household.

In the land of Uz there lived a man whose name was Job. This man was blameless and upright; he feared God and shunned evil. He had seven sons and three daughters, and he owned seven thousand sheep, three thousand camels, five hundred yoke of oxen and five hundred donkeys, and had a large number of servants. He was the greatest man among all the people of the East (Job 1:1-3).

The secret of Job's success both in the kingdom of God and in the world was that he watched over his household (family, business, and staff) and made sure that God remained his priority. Job built an altar to God and interceded at the altar for his family and business.

> His sons used to take turns holding feasts in their homes, and they would invite their three sisters to eat and drink with them. When a period of feasting had run its course, Job would send and have them purified. Early in the morning he would sacrifice a burnt offering for each of them, thinking, "Perhaps my children have sinned and cursed God in their hearts." This was Job's regular custom (Job 1:4-5).

Job was called the greatest man among all the people of the East because greatness is not just in possessions but in who you are before God. God is the only one who can pronounce eternal greatness. *"The fool says in his heart, 'There is no God.' They are corrupt, their deeds are vile; there is no one who does good"* (Psalm 14:1).

Religious altars are often established with spiritual intent by religious and occult groups. At religious altars, people establish a place of consecration to a **spiritual force**, giving it permission to release demonic power and influence in them, through them, in that place, and in that community. The altar establishes alliances, allegiances (promises to serve its mission), and authority for influence and transformation of that school, workplace, neighborhood, or community. An altar creates an open door to spiritual forces according to the intent and allegiance of the person who builds it. This is seen where communities are taken over by violence, prostitution (red light districts), occult districts, drug districts, and gang districts. A person or team intentionally marks and dedicates a territory for influence, control, and dominion. That person begin to evangelize, radicalize, and raise up teams to recruit, grow, and take over communities.

Satan is using Jesus' model of how to save the world to destroy the world.

THE POWER OF COMMUNITY ALTARS

The Bible gives us a glimpse of spiritual activity at an altar. Abraham had built a community altar at a place called Bethel.

> The Lord appeared to Abram and said, "To your offspring I will give this land." So he built an altar there to the Lord, who had appeared to him. From there he went on toward the hills east of Bethel and pitched his tent, with Bethel on the west and Ai on the east. There he built an altar to the Lord and called on the name of the Lord (Genesis 12:7,8).

This community altar was established by Abraham for a generational legacy. By faith he believed that his family would serve God and that his sons, grandsons, and their descendants would continue to be in God's family forever.

Hundreds of years later, after Abraham had died, his grandson Jacob was struggling with his faith, attitude, and purpose. He stole his brother's birthright and blessing and became a hunted fugitive who was threatened to be killed by his brother. After running from his brother for days, he stopped for the night to rest on the ground at Bethel and put a stone there under his head and began to sleep. It would be interesting to know if the stone he put under his head was one from the community altar that Abraham had built, because Jacob had an encounter with God in a dream. Altars were made of rough stones found on the ground. In his dream,

Jacob saw the activity and the work of God's angels at the consecrated place in Bethel. *"He had a dream in which he saw a stairway resting on the earth, with its top reaching to heaven, and the angels of God were ascending and descending on it"* (Genesis 28:11,12).

Jacob saw in His dream God standing above the land that was dedicated to Him at the community altar:

> There above it stood the Lord, and he said: "I am the Lord, the God of your father Abraham and the God of Isaac. I will give you and your descendants the land on which you are lying. Your descendants will be like the dust of the earth, and you will spread out to the west and to the east, to the north and to the south. All peoples on earth will be blessed through you and your offspring. I am with you and will watch over you wherever you go, and I will bring you back to this land. I will not leave you until I have done what I have promised you" (Genesis 28:13-15).

When parents and rulers on earth build community altars to God, the covenant includes generations and continues to fight for the legacy and declarations of the patriarch. Jacob awoke from his sleep and knew that he slept at the gate of Heaven: *"When Jacob awoke from his sleep, he thought, 'Surely the Lord is in this place, and I was not aware of it.' He was afraid and said, How awesome is this place! This is none other than the house of God; this is the gate of heaven'"* (Genesis 28:16-17). The community altar was still spiritually in place on earth and with access to the gate of Heaven.

When a spiritual altar is built unto God, it creates an opened gate, door, or portal into the realm of the spirit, for intentional access to God and His holy angels. It is built by faith for a personal encounter with God for the release of His power, peace, mercy, forgiveness, blessing, and kingdom to rule in our hearts, place, community, and nation. It is to establish the kingdom of God on earth.

A Community Altar

Hundreds of years later, the gate of Heaven that was opened by God to give Abraham and his descendants access was opened to Abraham's grandson, Jacob. Altars to our King of glory are powerful and with generational influence. Jacob claimed his family inheritance and renamed that community with the name Abraham had dedicated: *"Early the next morning Jacob took the stone he had placed under his head and set it up as a pillar and poured oil on top of it. He called that place Bethel, though the city used to be called Luz"* (Genesis 28:18-19). Wow! Altars to our King of glory are powerful and with generational influence, and when properly built, they will activate descendants to fight for their purpose.

Community altars are key to God's mission for community and societal transformation. In a time when our world is under siege by violent and corrupted principalities, God is saying to us, *"I will grant peace in the land, and you will lie down and no one will make you afraid. I will remove savage beasts from the land, and the sword will not pass through your country"* (Leviticus 26:6). Jesus Christ is the Prince of peace, the Savior of the world, the Healer of the sick and wounded, and the Source of eternal life for all the people of the world.

When a community altar to God is established in a school, workplace, or community, the powerful presence of Jesus Christ will neutralize the power of evil in one place at a time until the whole community is transformed by a spirit of peace, prosperity, and security. The power of the ark of God before the idol Dagon in its temple is seen:

> Then they carried the ark into Dagon's temple and set it beside Dagon. When the people of Ashdod rose early the next day, there was Dagon, fallen on his face on the ground before the ark of the Lord! They took Dagon and put him back in his place. But the following morning when they rose, there was Dagon, fallen on his face on the ground before the ark of the Lord! (1 Samuel 5:1-4).

The powerful presence of God is greater than all other powers. Wherever the presence of the Lord God abides (in a heart, home, church, school, workplace, community, or nation), by special invitation it is *blessed*.

ESTABLISHING A COMMUNITY ALTAR

A community altar is built like all altars to our King of glory. It is:

1. ***Spiritual not physical.*** We do not build a physical place or set up idols, candles, pictures of the dead, or any man-made furniture or symbol. Our worship to God is spiritual: *"Yet a time is coming and has now come when the true worshipers will worship the Father in spirit and truth, for they are the kind of worshipers the Father seeks. God is spirit, and his worshipers must worship in spirit and in truth"* (John 4:23-24).

2. ***Built intentionally.*** We intentionally invite Jesus Christ into our school, workplace, or community to establish His presence and kingdom in that place. Worship and prayers are offered up to God in exchange for His power and strength to be released to manifest in and through His servants in His mission to save our world and to bring His peace and prosperity in every community.

3. ***Built with expectations.*** *"The temple I am going to build will be great, because our God is greater than all other gods. But who is able to build a temple for him, since the heavens, even the highest heavens, cannot contain him? Who then am I to build a temple for him, except as a place to burn sacrifices before him?"* (2 Chronicles 2:5-6). Solomon established his kingdom by establishing a temple with the altar to God for worship, sacrifices, and offerings before Him. Solomon

remained successful as long as God remained His King of kings, and Israel remained in peace as long as God remained their Lord Most High.

4. ***Built as a place of prayer and intercession.*** *"I tell you the truth, whatever you bind on earth will be bound in heaven, and whatever you loose on earth will be loosed in heaven. Again, I tell you that if two of you on earth agree about anything you ask for, it will be done for you by my Father in heaven. For where two or three come together in my name, there am I with them"* (Matthew 18:18-20).

5. ***Built for kingdom revelation and government.*** When a community altar is built in a school or workplace, God is honored as the Source of wisdom, provision, protection, and prosperity. The kingdom of God is righteousness, peace, and joy in the Holy Spirit. Our world is crying and praying for peace. Peace has an Owner. The prophet Isaiah was given the revelation of the government and kingdom of Jesus: *"For to us a child is born, to us a son is given, and the government will be on his shoulders. And he will be called Wonderful Counselor, Mighty God, Everlasting Father, Prince of Peace"* (Isaiah 9:6). Peace will come to a community in one heart, one home, and one place to infuse and transform lives and the community. *"So Gideon built an altar to the Lord there and called it The Lord is Peace. To this day it stands in Ophrah of the Abiezrites"* (Judges 6:24). *"Thus Midian was subdued before the Israelites and did not raise its head again. During Gideon's lifetime, the land enjoyed peace forty years"* (Judges 8:28). A community altar to the Lord is powerful for prosperity and protection against evil.

6. ***Built by faith declaration.*** *"You will also declare a thing, And it will be established for you; So light will*

shine on your ways" (Job 22:28 NKJV). We know what we are doing, we say what we are doing, and we expect results. *"Now faith is the substance of things hoped for, the evidence of things not seen"* (Hebrews 11:1 NKJV).

BLESSING FOR SCHOOLS, WORKPLACES, AND ORGANIZATIONS WITH COMMUNITY ALTARS

I will grant peace in the land, and you will lie down and no one will make you afraid. I will remove savage beasts from the land, and the sword will not pass through your country (Leviticus 26:6).

He grants peace to your borders and satisfies you with the finest of wheat (Psalm 147:14).

Instead of bronze I will bring you gold, and silver in place of iron. Instead of wood I will bring you bronze, and iron in place of stones. I will make peace your governor and righteousness your ruler. No longer will violence be heard in your land, nor ruin or destruction within your borders, but you will call your walls Salvation and your gates Praise (Isaiah 60:17-18).

I will bless them and the places surrounding my hill. I will send down showers in season; there will be showers of blessing (Ezekiel 34:26).

The Lord will grant you abundant prosperity—in the fruit of your womb, the young of your livestock and the crops of your ground—in the land he swore to your forefathers to give you (Deuteronomy 28:11).

With me are riches and honor, enduring wealth and prosperity (Proverbs 8:18).

CHAPTER 7

A National Altar

> Then Noah built an altar to the Lord and...The Lord smelled the pleasing aroma and said in his heart: "Never again will I curse the ground because of man, even though every inclination of his heart is evil from childhood. And never again will I destroy all living creatures, as I have done" (Genesis 8:20-21).

A *national altar* to our King of glory, the Lord Jesus Christ, is built by a person with great authority in the kingdoms, governments, and nations of this world. Government leaders, presidents, prime ministers, kings, and chiefs are very powerful people as they can invite either God or evil principalities to take over and dominate their nations.

National altars are powerful, as seen in the national altar to the Lord that was built by Noah (see Genesis 8:20-21). One man's altar motivated God to reverse the curse on the earth and to make a vow that, regardless of the cycles of evil that will invade the earth, He will never again destroy all living creatures. National altars are powerful.

During Noah's time, the earth was at a dangerous tipping point of infusion of corruption and violence.

> Now the earth was corrupt in God's sight and was full of violence. God saw how corrupt the earth had become, for all the people on earth had corrupted their ways. So God said to Noah, "I am going to put an end to all people, for the earth is filled with violence because of them. I am surely going to destroy both them and the earth" (Genesis 6:11-13).

When communities and nations are infused with corruption, violence, and evil, they become unlivable by people. Demonic spirits of fear, violence, torment, and corruption cripple minds, torment hearts, possess lives, and dominate communities and nations.

Throughout the history of mankind, there have been many ruthless and cruel rulers who used violence, terror, and occult powers to gain control of people groups, communities, and nations. Their thirst for power, money, and subduing others was demonic and therefore never satisfied. They were driven to unconscionable and inhumane actions that had no limits. Their rule was characterized by political oppression and suppression, human rights abuses, religious persecution, ethnic persecution, tribal persecution, corrupted judicial killings, torture, forcing mass evacuations of cities, killing or displacing thousands of people, forced labor, slavery, or leaving a legacy of disease and poverty. Some caused millions of deaths and severe horror in humanity.

In a careful study of these ruthless leaders who were powerful to subdue communities and nations, it is seen that in them was a common trend of high-level superstition and suspicion, engagement with occult and spiritual forces, worship of idols, dependence on supernatural powers and spiritual forces of fear and torment. They were tormentors who themselves were tormented by their evil forces. They worshiped and offered sacrifices (often human) at community or national altars that they built in their official residences, palaces, or government buildings.

Spiritual thrones of powers are ruled through human agents who intentionally surrender their souls to demonic spiritual forces in exchange for power recognition. The world has seen the results of occult government. *"For all the gods of the nations are idols, but the Lord made the heavens"* (1 Chronicles 16:26). Now God will display His power and glory through great men and women in government leadership who will worship and exalt the Lord Jesus Christ as their King of kings and Lord of lords: *"Let the heavens rejoice, let the earth be glad; let them say among the nations, 'The Lord reigns!'"* (1 Chronicles 16:31).

A national altar to the Lord Jesus Christ is built to intentionally establish His presence for His power, peace, mercy, government, and kingdom to rule in that nation. God's invitation to leaders of nations is this: *"Ask of me, and I will make the nations your inheritance, the ends of the earth your possession"* (Psalm 2:8). Jesus Christ, the King of glory, is looking for world leaders through whom He can display His glory. *"I will display my glory among the nations"* (Ezekiel 39:21). Jesus Christ is looking for leaders through whom He can be a blessing to the nations. CHAYIL glory is the manifested power and glory of our Lord Jesus Christ *in* and *through* His servants. At the national altar, Christian leaders will worship God, privately and publicly declaring their alliance and allegiance to Jesus Christ: *"Therefore I will praise you, O Lord, among the nations; I will sing praises to your name. He gives his king great victories; he shows unfailing kindness to his anointed, to David and his descendants forever"* (2 Samuel 22:50-51).

The result of a national altar to the Lord Jesus Christ in a nation is national blessing on the people and land of that nation: *"Blessed is the nation whose God is the Lord, the people he chose for his inheritance"* (Psalm 33:12). The fruit of a blessed nation is peace, prosperity, unity, blessing upon the produce and products of the land, great alliances with other nations, respect from other nations, and security at its borders.

A nation that makes the kingdom of the Lord Jesus Christ its priority will be an exalted nation: *"Righteousness exalts a nation, but sin is a disgrace to any people"* (Proverbs 14:34).

Throughout history, we see the rise and fall of nations. In our sophisticated world, evil spirituality is being exalted by media and Christianity is being undermined and even persecuted in the guise of tolerance. From history, however, we can see that economic, social, and political problems are often symptoms of a spiritual decline of a nation: *"Righteousness exalts a nation, but sin is a disgrace to any people"* (Proverb 14:34). History is a great teacher. As the philosopher Hegel said, "What experience and history teach us is this: that people and government never have learned anything from history or acted on principles deduced from it."

Historians show that great civilizations in the world went through cyclical stages from birth to decline to death, and we can see that in "superpowers" such as the Babylonians, the Assyrians, the Greeks, and Romans. It is said that the average time span of great civilizations is about two hundred years. Professor Alex Tyler, a Scottish historian, says that there are ten stages through which civilizations go through from their birth to their decline and death. The first stage moves from bondage to spiritual faith; the second from spiritual faith to great courage; the third from great courage to liberty; the fourth from liberty to abundance; the fifth from abundance to selfishness; the sixth from selfishness to complacency; the seventh stage from complacency to apathy; the eighth from apathy to moral decay; the ninth from moral decay to dependence; and the tenth and last stage moves from dependence to bondage.

Interestingly enough, these ten stages are similar to the stages described in the historical Book of Judges in the Old Testament. In Judges, we read of the chaotic period in the history of Israel between Joshua's death and her transition into becoming a kingdom under the leadership of King Saul. Without the godly and devoted leadership of Joshua, the Israelites went through cycles of abundance, instability, and moral depravity to worshiping false gods and oppression.

To punish the people, God removed His protection from them and they were subdued by enemy nations. In their

A National Altar

distress, the people prayed, repented, and cried out to God for help. God answered their cries for mercy by raising up a judge whom He glorified as their deliverer. But the cycles would start again.

> The Israelites did evil in the eyes of the Lord; they forgot the Lord their God and served the Baals and the Asherahs. The anger of the Lord burned against Israel so that he sold them into the hands of Cushan-Rishathaim king of Aram Naharaim, to whom the Israelites were subject for eight years. But when they cried out to the Lord, he raised up for them a deliverer, Othniel son of Kenaz, Caleb's younger brother, who saved them (Judges 3:7-9).

Without a strong godly leader like Joshua to maintain the national altar to the Lord God, to encourage the priestly government of worship, offerings, and obedience to God's principles and practices, the people of Israel became tolerant of many gods and eventually joined others in the worship of false gods. It was a continual cycle of faithfulness to God and security, obedience to God and prosperity, then after a period, the people once again forgot God and started again the cycle of unfaithfulness that led to punishment and yet another cycle. Throughout the Book of Judges, the cycle of sin to punishment to repentance to deliverance runs seven times, beginning with the refrain, *"Again the Israelites did evil in the eyes of the Lord"* (Judges 3:12). This went on for a period of about 300 years in a progression from bondage to liberty back to bondage. One generation broke the chains of bondage only to have the next generation, through ignorance, tolerance, apathy, and deception, fall into rebellion and demonic slavery.

When government leaders despise and reject the Word of God, the Bible describes it as the sin of witchcraft or occult practice: *"For rebellion is as the sin of witchcraft, and stubbornness is as iniquity and idolatry. Because you have rejected the word of the Lord, He also has rejected you from being king"* (1 Samuel 15:23 NKJV). When government leaders honor God and in humility ask Him to lead and rule their nation through them, God comes with His kingdom of righteousness, peace, and joy and with His assignment to destroy the works of the evil one. The power of Jesus Christ is greater than all power of evil. The power and glory of Jesus Christ in His servants is greater than all evil power and opposition: *"You are of God, little children, and have overcome them, because He who is in you is greater than he who is in the world"* (1 John 4:4 NKJV).

God's covenant with Abraham is for all government leaders who make a covenant with the Lord Jesus Christ and give Him permission to rule that nation through them:

> The Lord had said to Abram, "Leave your country, your people and your father's household and go to the land I will show you. I will make you into a great nation and I will bless you; I will make your name great, and you will be a blessing. I will bless those who bless you, and whoever curses you I will curse; and all peoples on earth will be blessed through you" (Genesis 12:1-3).

"He [Jesus Christ] redeemed us in order that the blessing given to Abraham might come to the Gentiles through Christ Jesus, so that by faith we might receive the promise of the Spirit" (Galatians 3:14-15). *"So those who have faith are blessed along with Abraham, the man of faith"* (Galatians 3:9). *"The Lord will protect him and preserve his life; he will bless him in the land and not surrender him to the desire of his foes"* (Psalm 41:2). *"The Lord will send a blessing on your barns and on everything you put your hand to. The Lord your God will bless you in the land he is giving you"* (Deuteronomy 28:8).

A national altar is built like all altars to our King of glory. It is:

A National Altar

1. ***Spiritual not physical.*** We do not build a physical place or set up idols, candles, pictures of the dead, or any man-made furniture or symbol. Our worship to God is spiritual: *"Yet a time is coming and has now come when the true worshipers will worship the Father in spirit and truth, for they are the kind of worshipers the Father seeks. God is spirit, and his worshipers must worship in spirit and in truth"* (John 4:23-24).

2. ***Built intentionally.*** We intentionally invite Jesus Christ into our nation to establish His presence and kingdom. Worship and prayers are offered up to God in exchange for His power and strength to be released to manifest in and through His servants in His mission to save our world and to bring His peace and prosperity in every nation. *"Then the land will yield its harvest, and God, our God, will bless us"* (Psalm 67:6).

3. ***Built with expectations.*** *"Then God said to Jacob, 'Go up to Bethel and settle there, and build an altar there to God, who appeared to you when you were fleeing from your brother Esau'"* (Genesis 35:1). God coached Jacob on how to secure His continued presence, power, and prosperity in the land that God gave him to settle. *"Jacob and all the people with him came to Luz (that is, Bethel) in the land of Canaan. There he built an altar, and he called the place El Bethel, because it was there that God revealed himself to him when he was fleeing from his brother"* (Genesis 35:6-7). El Bethel means the house or territory of the strong (CHAYIL) God. God was his Almighty God, Omnipotent God, and King of glory.

4. ***Built as a place of prayer and intercession.*** *"I tell you the truth, whatever you bind on earth will be bound in heaven, and whatever you loose on earth will be loosed in heaven. Again, I tell you that if two of*

you on earth agree about anything you ask for, it will be done for you by my Father in heaven. For where two or three come together in my name, there am I with them" (Matthew 18:18-20).

5. **Built for kingdom revelation and government.** *"O Lord Almighty, blessed is the man who trusts in you"* (Psalm 84:12). *"Blessed is the man who does not walk in the counsel of the wicked or stand in the way of sinners or sit in the seat of mockers. But his delight is in the law of the Lord, and on his law he meditates day and night. He is like a tree planted by streams of water, which yields its fruit in season and whose leaf does not wither. Whatever he does prospers"* (Psalm 1:1-3). God is our source of wisdom. When God finds humble and gracious leaders like Solomon, He bless them with godly wisdom (superior CHAYIL—powerful wisdom) resulting in holistic prosperity and lasting legacy. Gideon built and named his national altar: *"So Gideon built an altar to the Lord there and called it The Lord is Peace. To this day it stands in Ophrah of the Abiezrites"* (Judges 6:24). *"Thus Midian was subdued before the Israelites and did not raise its head again. During Gideon's lifetime, the land enjoyed peace forty years"* (Judges 8:28). A community altar to the Lord is powerful for prosperity and protection against evil.

6. **Built by faith declaration.** *"You will also declare a thing, And it will be established for you; So light will shine on your ways"* (Job 22:28 NKJV). We know what we are doing, we say what we are doing, and we expect results. *"Now faith is the substance of things hoped for, the evidence of things not seen"* (Hebrews 11:1 NKJV).

God is looking for committed men and women to whom He will give the kingdoms of this world: *"The decision is announced by messengers, the holy ones declare the ver-*

dict, so that the living may know that the Most High is sovereign over the kingdoms of men and gives them to anyone he wishes and sets over them the lowliest of men" (Daniel 4:17). When He finds committed and trustworthy hearts, there is no limit of manifested glory in and through them: *"The eyes of the Lord search the whole earth in order to strengthen those whose hearts are fully committed to him. What a fool you have been! From now on, you will be at war"* (2 Chronicles 16:9). May God find you!

CHAPTER 8

The Church Altar

One day Peter and John were going up to the temple at the time of prayer—at three in the afternoon (Acts 3:1).

I n the Old Testament, the law that was given to Moses at Mount Sinai included the building of physical altars for the offering of sacrifices of animals, grains, and incense and other practices that were types and shadows leading to the work of Jesus Christ on the altar of God called the cross. The Church is an altar, and God's altar for the world is the cross. The Church of Jesus Christ is spiritual: *"As you come to him, the living Stone—rejected by men but chosen by God and precious to him—you also, like living stones, are being built into a spiritual house to be a holy priesthood, offering spiritual sacrifices acceptable to God through Jesus Christ"* (1 Peter 2:4-5). Metaphorically, Jesus Christ is the Living Stone, the Chief Cornerstone in His Church, and we are the living stones that make up the building of God's spiritual house. The Church is universal, one Church at several locations. The church is also a physical building that is dedicated for corporate worship and is a spiritual altar where believers come together to bring their tithes and offerings, for prayer and intercession, to participate in the sacraments of the church, and for a spiritual encounter with God to receive miracles and blessing.

At the altar of the church, we remember God's altar for us, the cross. On the cross, Jesus became the sacrificial Lamb of God who was slain for all the sins of the world. *"The next day*

John saw Jesus coming toward him and said, 'Look, the Lamb of God, who takes away the sin of the world!'" (John 1:29). We are cautioned not to undermine the work of Jesus Christ on the cross and the privilege of our Christian faith by observing practices that are no longer necessary. Under the New Covenant, it is no longer scriptural to build physical altars of stone, as Jesus Christ and His believers are the stones where Jesus became our sacrifice, and our lives are a sacrifice to Him. We no longer offer sacrifices of animals, grains, or incense and our worship is in spirit and in truth: *"Yet a time is coming and has now come when the true worshipers will worship the Father in spirit and truth, for they are the kind of worshipers the Father seeks. God is spirit, and his worshipers must worship in spirit and in truth"* (John 4:23-24).

However, the principles and power of building by faith a spiritual altar to our King of glory, Jesus Christ, still remain. A spiritual altar is an open portal into the realm of the spirit to intentionally be in the presence of the Lord Jesus Christ for worship, prayer, communion, confession, consecration, covenant, intercession, exchange, offerings, receiving revelation and instructions, and to receive fresh power and glory to go forward as servants of God. In prayer, we enter His presence by faith for a personal encounter with God for the release of His forgiveness, mercy, peace, and blessing and for the kingdom to rule in our hearts. Our worship at the altar is in spirit (our hearts connecting with the Spirit of God) and in truth (with a pure agenda to glorify God in His presence and in our lives).

Jesus tells us how to build a spiritual altar to attract His presence: *"For where two or three come together in my name, there am I with them"* (Matthew 18:20). In corporate worship, we come together to worship Jesus Christ in His Church. Jesus oversees everything in His Church, including worship, offerings (financial: tithes and offerings), service, teaching, revelation, and celebrations. *"And God placed all things under his*

The Church Altar

feet and appointed him to be head over everything for the church, which is his body, the fullness of him who fills everything in every way" (Ephesians 1:22-23). The birthing of His Church and its government, operations, eldership, worship, prayer, and intercession is given great importance by God in the New Testament. The Church is mentioned throughout the New Testament from the first book, Matthew, to the last book of the Bible and in the last chapter of the Book of Revelation.

In corporate worship, as believers gather in church for corporate praise and worship, God inhabits the praise of His believers. God is omnipresent: He dwells in hearts, in His temple or church, and everywhere He is invited to establish His kingdom. The word *dwell* means, therefore, that wherever God is honored, worshiped, and obeyed becomes a place for His awesome presence and manifested glory. Our heart can be His altar and we can by faith create a spiritual altar at our home, school, workplace, community, and nation, welcoming and establishing God's spiritual kingdom on earth.

The church altar is a meeting place with God and people:

1. **To offer God worship.** God seeks personal and corporate worship that is due to His holy name. *"Yet a time is coming and has now come when the true worshipers will worship the Father in spirit and truth, for they are the kind of worshipers the Father seeks. God is spirit, and his worshipers must worship in spirit and in truth"* (John 4:23-24). In corporate worship, God finds a resting place and receives our worship as sweet-smelling incense. In worship, we serve God and satisfy His heart. In God's awesome presence, we exalt Him for who He is, what He has done, and what He can do. We offer sacrifices of praise, the fruit of our lips, giving thanks in the presence of His holiness.

    The Church is the altar for the assembly of believers: *"Sing to the Lord a new song, his praise in the assembly of the saints"* (Psalm 149:1). *"Let us go to his dwelling place; let us worship at his footstool—arise, O Lord, and come to your resting place,* **you and the ark of your might.** *May your priests be clothed with righteousness; may your saints sing for joy"* (Psalm 132:7-9 emphasis added). The presence of God is symbolized by His ark and His altar where demons are neutralized by His CHAYIL glory, captives are set free, stubborn sickness is healed, and believers are strengthened with His joy. As we give God joy by worshiping Him, His joy becomes our strength.

2. **To bring tithes and offerings.** Bringing our tithes and offerings to the assembly of God is a command of God to His saints.

> "Will a man rob God? Yet you rob me. But you ask, 'How do we rob you?' In tithes and offerings. You are under a curse—the whole nation of you—because you are robbing me. Bring the whole tithe into the storehouse, that there may be food in my house. Test me in this," says the Lord Almighty, "and see if I will not throw open the floodgates of heaven and pour out so much blessing that you will not have room enough for it" (Malachi 3:8-10).

The tithe and offerings are used to strengthen the priesthood of God that must remain forever.

The church is the lighthouse in communities and nations. It shows the heart of people and a nation that God is an important priority for families. Teaching and equipping believers are vital to the life and priesthood of God. His church is His house for saving souls, transforming lives, and influencing communities and nations. Tithes and offerings when brought to His church altar break the power of darkness in lives, reverse curses, and mobilize God to fight for us. *"Ascribe to the Lord the glory due his name. Bring an offering and come before him; worship the Lord in the splendor of his holiness"* (1 Chronicles 16:29).

3. **For blessing.** Children are blessed and people are blessed at the church altar. The anointing with oil at the church altar releases the priestly blessing that was commanded by God. Children are dedicated to the Lord and blessed at the church altar. God is generational and always includes children as part of the sustainability plan of His kingdom. *"The children of your servants will live in your presence; their descendants will be established before you"* (Psalm 102:28).

4. **For marriages.** Marriage was the first sacrament created by God, and He performed the first marriage of the man and the woman, Adam and Eve, in the garden of Eden. Marriage is sacred and powerful, when it is done by faith in God, God blesses the union of the man and woman to become one in destiny. The marriage becomes the birthing place for God's children and the future of His priesthood, His kingdom, and His Church. God's Church is one family of families.

5. **For praying for the sick.** There is a special power that is released to the sick when they are prayed for at the church altar. *"Is anyone among you sick? Let him call for the elders of the church, and let them pray over him, anointing him with oil in the name of the Lord. And the prayer of faith will save the sick, and the Lord will raise him up. And if he has committed sins, he will be forgiven"* (James 5:14-15 NKJV).

6. **For intercession.** Jesus was very specific about one of the great importance of His Church, His house: *"It is written...'My house will be called a house of prayer,' but*

you are making it a 'den of robbers'" (Matthew 21:13). Jesus also told us that His Church is also called to pray specifically for nations: *"And as he taught them, he said, 'Is it not written: "My house will be called a house of prayer for all nations"? But you have made it "a den of robbers""'* (Mark 11:17).

Corporate prayer is powerful because it involves the law of synergy that can make prayer more impactful. *"How could one man chase a thousand, or two put ten thousand to flight, unless their Rock had sold them, unless the Lord had given them up?"* (Deuteronomy 32:30). Numbers are so important to God that in His Bible is a book of Numbers. God's Church is one of the armies of the Lord. EL CHAYIL is Lord of armies, King of glory, Lord of wealth. The Bible describes Jesus Christ in a mode of war: *"He is dressed in a robe dipped in blood, and his name is the Word of God.* **The armies of heaven** *were following him, riding on white horses and dressed in fine linen, white and clean"* (Revelation 19:13-14 emphasis added). Our Lord of Armies has His armies of angels and His armies of believing worshiping warriors, His Church.

He has given us instructions on how to create an altar for His presence in intercession: *"For where two or three come together in my name, there am I with them."* He tells us about our power and authority in intercession: *"I tell you the truth, whatever you bind on earth will be bound in heaven, and whatever you loose on earth will be loosed in heaven."* He tells us about the power of corporate agreement and unity in intercession: *"Again, I tell you that if two of you on earth agree about anything you ask for, it will be done for you by my Father in heaven"* (Matthew 18:18-20). Corporate prayer and intercession at the church altar is powerful to chase and neutralize demonic forces: *"Five of you will chase a hundred, and a hundred of you will chase ten thousand, and your enemies will fall by the sword before you"* (Leviticus 26:8).

7. **For the sacrament of communion.** Jesus told us to keep the cross before us by partaking of communion regularly:

   > For I received from the Lord what I also passed on to you: The Lord Jesus, on the night he was betrayed, took bread, and when he had given thanks, he broke it and said, "This is my body, which is for you; do this in remembrance of me." In the same way, after supper he took the cup, saying, "This cup is the new covenant in my blood; do this, whenever you drink it, in remembrance of me." For whenever you eat this bread and drink this cup, you proclaim the Lord's death until he comes (1 Corinthians 11:23-26).

   The cross is a weapon of spiritual warfare, and it cancels every curse and everything that is written or spoken against you every time you partake of communion. The blood of Jesus cries out for vengeance against your and His enemies every time you partake of communion. The stripes on His back cry out for healing every time you partake of communion. Your sins are forgiven every time you partake of communion. Partaking in communion at His church altar is powerful.

8. **For fellowship.** *"They devoted themselves to the apostles' teaching and to the fellowship, to the breaking of bread and to prayer"* (Acts 2:42). *"And let us consider one another in order to stir up love and good works, not forsaking the assembling of ourselves together, as is the manner of some, but exhorting one*

another, and so much the more as you see the Day approaching" (Hebrew 10:24-25).

9. **For His manifested glory.** CHAYIL glory is the manifested power and glory of our Lord Jesus Christ *in* and *through* His servants. *"Now to him who is able to do immeasurably more than all we ask or imagine, according to his power that is at work within us, to him be glory in the church and in Christ Jesus throughout all generations, for ever and ever! Amen"* (Ephesians 3:20-21). God receives glory in His Church when His saints come together in worship and to serve Him by serving others. At the church altar, believers come together with expectancy for teaching, encouragement, the Word of the Lord, miracles, and fellowship. The Church is the manifested glory of the Lord Jesus Christ, showing that God is still in the midst of His people in corporate worship and His importance in our community and nation.

CHAPTER 9

The Altar of God, the Cross

For Christ, our Passover lamb, has been sacrificed (1 Corinthians 5:7).

Even as we share about the power of altars, the most powerful altar is the cross of Jesus Christ. *"The next day John saw Jesus coming toward him and said, 'Look, the Lamb of God, who takes away the sin of the world!'"* (John 1:29). The altars of the Old Testament always pointed to the cross of Jesus Christ, when He would become the perfect and ultimate sacrifice for the sins of the world. So powerful was the altar of the cross that He is revered and worshiped in Heaven forever as the Lamb who was slain:

> And every creature which is in heaven and on the earth and under the earth and such as are in the sea, and all that are in them, I heard saying: "Blessing and honor and glory and power Be to Him who sits on the throne, And to the Lamb, forever and ever!" Then the four living creatures said, "Amen!" And the twenty-four elders fell down and worshiped Him who lives forever and ever (Revelation 5:13-14 NKJV).

Jesus was crucified on a cross, His death was intentional, and the way He died was purposeful.

> Finally Pilate handed him over to them to be crucified. So the soldiers took charge of Jesus. Carrying his own cross, he went out to the place of the Skull (which in Aramaic is called Golgotha). Here they crucified him,

and with him two others—one on each side and Jesus in the middle (John 19:16-18).

Jesus did not die of a heart attack or by an electric chair, but on a wooden cross where His blood flowed on the hill of Calvary. His death was bloody, shameful, physically and emotionally torturous, and slow, as He intentionally took the penalty of *all* the sins of the world and shed enough blood to erase every record of our debts, trespasses, and sins. Jesus fulfilled the requirements of atonement and forgiveness of sins that the altars of the Old Covenant tried to fulfill.

THE SACRIFICIAL SYSTEM THROUGH MOSES

Under the Old Covenant in the Old Testament, God through Moses created a sacrificial system as a means for Israel to be in covenant with God and maintain relationship with Him:

> Then the Lord said to Moses, "Tell the Israelites this: 'You have seen for yourselves that I have spoken to you from heaven: Do not make any gods to be alongside me; do not make for yourselves gods of silver or gods of gold. **Make an altar of earth for me and sacrifice on it your burnt offerings and fellowship offerings, your sheep and goats and your cattle. Wherever I cause my name to be honored, I will come to you and bless you.** If you make an altar of stones for me, do not build it with dressed stones, for you will defile it if you use a tool on it" (Exodus 20:22-26).

The power and principle behind altars was for God's people to seek Him in relationship and to be blessed by Him. The altar itself was symbolic; more important was faith in God, the worship of God, and obedience to God.

The sacrificial system satisfied three main purposes:

The Altar of God

1. ***Consecration.*** Israel was to be set apart, dedicated, "holy" unto God. Worship of other gods or being involved in pagan practices, rituals, and lifestyles were prohibited. God wanted a people for His very own and not to be shared with Satan or idols. *"Now if you obey me fully and keep my covenant, then out of all nations you will be my treasured possession. Although the whole earth is mine, you will be for me a kingdom of priests and a holy nation.' These are the words you are to speak to the Israelites"* (Exodus 19:5-6). When we build spiritual altars in prayer and intercession, we are consecrating ourselves to Jesus Christ to serve Him in worship and obedience to His Word. Our lives are set apart for service unto Him and for the cause of His Church, His kingdom, and to fill the earth with His glory.

2. ***Expiation.*** *Expiation* means atonement for sins and satisfying the penalty of death for sins. The Bible states that sin deserves the death penalty: *"For the wages of sin is death, but the gift of God is eternal life in Christ Jesus our Lord"* (Romans 6:23). In the Old Covenant, animals were slaughtered and burnt as sin offerings on altars symbolizing the suffering, death, penalty, and payment for the sins of the one making the sacrificial offering. The legal requirement for an offence committed was satisfied on the altar. The blood and flesh of an animal was offered to God as a "substitute payment" for sin. The death penalty was taken by an animal instead of the human offender.

According to God's command, the animal sacrificed had to be without blemish and physically perfect in age and condition. God was careful about details as the sacrificial system was pointing toward the ultimate sacrifice of His perfect Son, Jesus: *"The law is only a shadow of the good things that are coming—not the realities themselves"* (Hebrews 10:1).

In the atonement festivals, two goats were used to satisfy the redemption of sin. One goat was slaughtered and its blood placed on the mercy seat in the Holy of Holies, symbolizing that the sins of the offender was paid for, covered by the blood of the animal, and the person was now at peace with God. With the second goat, called the "scapegoat," the priest would symbolically lay his hand on the head of the goat and confer the sins of the people onto the goat. The scapegoat would then be let loose to run away into the wilderness as a symbol that the sin of people was removed and no longer with them. Guilt was appeased, and the death penalty for sin was satisfied.

3. **Propitiation.** This is the result of expiation. God was satisfied that the offender was truly sorry for his sins and showed his repentance by offering a sacrifice for the atonement of his sins. God no longer looked at the offender as guilty because his sins were covered by the blood of the animal and therefore God's grace and mercy is given. The symbolic acts of physical altars and sacrifices were all shadows leading to the work on the altar of the cross by Jesus Christ.

In the first mention of the word *offering* in the Bible or the implication of sacrifices, we see where animal sacrifice with the shedding of blood was looked upon favorably by God: *"In the course of time Cain brought some of the fruits of the soil as an offering to the Lord. But Abel brought fat portions from some of the firstborn of his flock. The Lord looked with favor on Abel and his offering"* (Genesis 4:3-4). Blood was a symbol of life, and the shedding of blood was therefore the offering of one's life. Under the sacrificial system, the life of an animal was offered to preserve the life of an offender, pointing to the time when Jesus would offer His life on the cross for the sins of the world.

THE ALTAR OF GOD

God's ultimate love for humanity was expressed in the sacrificial offering of His Son, Jesus.

> For God so loved the world that he gave his one and only Son, that whoever believes in him shall not perish but have eternal life. For God did not send his Son into the world to condemn the world, but to save the world through him. Whoever believes in him is not condemned, but whoever does not believe stands condemned already because he has not believed in the name of God's one and only Son (John 3:16-18).

Jesus gave His life so that we can have eternal life. Jesus suffered and died on the cross to satisfy the penalty of the sins of the world. The power of the love of Jesus is shown in the power of His cross. *"I have been crucified with Christ and I no longer live, but Christ lives in me. The life I live in the body, I live by faith in the Son of God, who loved me and gave himself for me"* (Galatians 2:20). What awesome manner of love the Father bestowed upon us to sacrifice His only begotten Son for us, and what awesome love Jesus Christ, Son of God, has for us to give His life for us while we were sinners.

When Moses was building the tabernacle, God told Him to build an altar made of wood, pointing to the altar of God, the cross, which would be made of wood. *"Build an altar of acacia wood, three cubits high; it is to be square, five cubits long and five cubits wide"* (Exodus 27:1). Jesus fully satisfied the law of sacrifice, paid the full penalty for all the sins of the world, appeased the heart of His Father for the judgment of sin, and in addition, broke the curse of mankind and healed all sickness and diseases. Awesome God. The sacrificial system through Moses was only temporary and was superseded by the sacrificial death of Jesus on the cross.

JESUS SATISFIED THE LAW OF THE SACRIFICIAL SYSTEM

1. **A perfect animal.** The animals that were sacrificed in the Old Covenant had to be perfect in age and condition. *"This is a requirement of the law that the Lord has commanded: Tell the Israelites to bring you a red heifer without defect or blemish and that has never been under a yoke"* (Numbers 19:1-2). The perfection of the animal pointed to the perfect Lamb of God who would be slain for the sins of the world. *"God made him who had no sin to be sin for us, so that in him we might become the righteousness of God"* (2 Corinthians 5:21). The perfection of Jesus as the sacrificial Lamb, slain for the sins of the world, made us righteous before God and with the ability to come before His holy presence without fear and guilt. Only the high priest could approach God's presence in the ark of the tabernacle and only once per year. God's presence was feared and revered. To unlawfully approach God's presence would result in death. God is holy, and only holiness could survive the power of His glory. To approach His holy presence, we now come to Him in the righteousness of Jesus Christ, the perfect Son of God.

2. **The shedding of blood.** An animal had to be slaughtered and its blood offered at the mercy seat in the Holy of Holies. *"The law requires that nearly everything be cleansed with blood, and without the shedding of blood there is no forgiveness"* (Hebrews 9:22). Jesus suffered a cruel and torturous death with His blood shed during His torture and on the cross. *"The blood of goats and bulls and the ashes of a heifer sprinkled on those who are ceremonially unclean sanctify them so that they are outwardly clean. How much more, then, will the blood of Christ, who through the eternal Spirit offered himself*

unblemished to God, cleanse our consciences from acts that lead to death, so that we may serve the living God!" (Hebrews 9:13-14). The power of the blood of Jesus is that it not only "covers" our sins, but it erases and wipes out our sins and we receive God's forgiveness. *"In him we have redemption through his blood, the forgiveness of sins, in accordance with the riches of God's grace"* (Ephesians 1:6-7).

3. **The wooden cross.** The cross was an instrument of torture for the vilest criminal. It was painful, public, and shameful. It displayed the curse that was deserved by criminals. The wooden cross was therefore symbolic and very powerful: *"Christ redeemed us from the **curse** of the law by becoming a **curse** for us, for it is written: 'Cursed is everyone who is hung on a tree.' He redeemed us in order that the blessing given to Abraham might come to the Gentiles through Christ Jesus, so that by faith we might receive the promise of the Spirit"* (Galatians 3:13-14 emphasis added).

Apostle Paul gloried in the symbol of the cross. The cross is a symbol of victory and wisdom to all who believe in Jesus Christ. *"For the message of the cross is foolishness to those who are perishing, but to us who are being saved it is the power of God. For it is written: 'I will destroy the wisdom of the wise; the intelligence of the intelligent I will frustrate'"* (1 Corinthians 1:18-19). Paul's power and the main message of the power of Jesus Christ was His cross: *"When I came to you, brothers, I did not come with eloquence or superior wisdom as I proclaimed to you the testimony about God. For I resolved to know nothing while I was with you except Jesus Christ and him crucified"* (1 Corinthians 2:1-2). The crucifixion of Jesus Christ on a cross is the gospel and power of salvation.

OUR ALTAR OF VICTORY

Paul talks about the cross of Jesus Christ as our altar of victory and a weapon of spiritual warfare:

> When you were dead in your sins and in the uncircumcision of your sinful nature, God made you alive with Christ. He forgave us all our sins, having canceled the written code, with its regulations, that was against us and that stood opposed to us; he took it away, nailing it to the cross. And having disarmed the powers and authorities, he made a public spectacle of them, triumphing over them by the cross (Colossians 2:13-15).

Through the cross, all our sins are forgiven, so the cross gave us victory over sins. Not only because of the cross are our sins forgiven, but also we have power to resist sin and the devil because of the power of the cross.

The victory of the altar of God, His cross, includes:

1. ***Forgiveness of sins.*** The written laws, codes, and regulations under the sacrificial system of Moses were a constant reminder of how imperfect people are and how impossible it is to be holy before God. People lived under "sin-consciousness" and with fear of being in the presence of God. The Bible confirms that we are all sinners: *"If we claim to be without sin, we deceive ourselves and the truth is not in us"* (1 John 1:8). The sin factor is something that all human beings have to deal with and live with the necessity of continual forgiveness. Without the cross, people are trapped by the horrors of guilt, condemnation, and shame. Without the cross, there is no victory over sin. *"But thanks be to God! He gives us the victory through our Lord Jesus Christ"* (1 Corinthians 15:57). It was as if Jesus asked an angel to write all our sins on miles of paper and then He took it and put it in His hands so that they were

The Altar of God

nailed to the cross. His nailed scarred hands and feet are memories of our freedom and victory by His cross.

2. **Freedom from the bondage of the law.** All the written laws, codes, and regulations were cancelled, meaning there were no longer able to be used against us. The new law of grace is now applied. *"In him we have redemption through his blood, the forgiveness of sins, in accordance with the riches of God's grace"* (Ephesians 1:7). Hallelujah, for the Son has set us free.

3. **Neutralized Satanic forces.** *"And having disarmed the powers and authorities, he made a public spectacle of them, triumphing over them by the cross"* (Colossians 2:15). The military terms used here shows the spiritual battle of Jesus Christ on His cross and in the grave as He disarmed evil forces at all levels. Satan was discredited by Jesus before his demons. He made a public spectacle of the weakness of Satan before Jesus Christ, the Almighty Savior of the world. Jesus Christ remains our victorious conqueror of Satan, death, and the grave, and because He lives, we too shall live. Because of His victory, we too shall have victory in our battles for the continuance of His manifested glory on earth.

4. **Restored power and authority to believers in Christ.** Jesus died on the cross, went to Hades, and stripped Satan of the power and authority that he stole from Adam and Eve. By the power of the cross, Christians are now restored to the glory of mankind in the beginning with power and dominion to create and rule the world.

> Then God said, "Let Us make man in Our image, according to Our likeness; let them have dominion over the fish of the sea, over the birds of the air, and over the cattle, over all the earth and over every creeping thing that creeps on the

earth." So God created man in His own image; in the image of God He created him; male and female He created them. Then God blessed them, and God said to them, "Be fruitful and multiply; fill the earth and subdue it; have dominion over the fish of the sea, over the birds of the air, and over every living thing that moves on the earth" (Genesis 1:26-28 NKJV).

Jesus Christ won back the keys of His kingdom with its power, authority, and glory and gave them to His Church and glorified believers. *"And I tell you that you are Peter, and on this rock I will build my church, and the gates of Hades will not overcome it. I will give you the keys of the kingdom of heaven; whatever you bind on earth will be bound in heaven, and whatever you loose on earth will be loosed in heaven"* (Matthew 16:18-19).

5. ***Unity in the family of God.*** Jews and Gentiles are unified as one family, one people, under God our Father:

> For he himself is our peace, who has made the two one and has destroyed the barrier, the dividing wall of hostility, by abolishing in his flesh the law with its commandments and regulations. His purpose was to create in himself **one new man out of the two**, thus making peace, and in this one body to reconcile both of them to God through the cross, by which he put to death their hostility. He came and preached peace to you who were far away and peace to those who were near. For through him we both have access to the Father by one Spirit (Ephesians 2:14-18 emphasis added).

The wall of hostility between Jews and Gentiles was broken down by the cross of Jesus, son of David, son of Abraham.

The Church of Jesus Christ, our Messiah, is the continuation of the covenant of God that He made with Abraham: *"He redeemed us in order that the blessing given to Abraham might come to the Gentiles through Christ Jesus, so that by faith we might receive the promise of the Spirit"* (Galatians 3:14). The covenant blessing of Abraham and the covenant glory of David is now with Jews and Gentiles as the blessed family of God. This miracle that was worked on the cross was the fulfillment of the desire of our Father's heart. Jesus Christ is the Savior of all mankind, and His wish is that none should perish. God loves all the people of the world. In unity, Jews and Gentiles can now fight the spiritual enemies of God, that is, Satan and his demons. Even as God passionately loves the world, we are now experiencing in our world the evil, violent passion of Satan to destroy people and our world. Jews and Gentiles as *one* man and *one* family of faith, purpose, vision, and passion can pray together for the salvation of our world and for peace in our world.

On the altar of the cross of Jesus Christ, prophecies were fulfilled. The death of Jesus on the cross was not an accident, it was intentional and promised by God: *"Men of Israel, listen to this: Jesus of Nazareth was a man accredited by God to you by miracles, wonders and signs, which God did among you through him, as you yourselves know. This man was handed over to you by God's set purpose and foreknowledge; and you, with the help of wicked men, put him to death by nailing him to the cross"* (Acts 2:22-23). Jews and Gentiles crucified Jesus on the cross as prophesied in the Old Testament. It was God's intent and design. Isaiah prophesied that He was brought as a lamb to the slaughter (Isaiah 53:7); David prophesied His betrayal (Psalm 41:9); Zechariah prophesied that Jesus would be forsaken by His disciples and sold for thirty pieces of silver

(Zechariah 13:7; 11:12); and both Isaiah and David prophesied that Jesus' body would be mutilated (Isaiah 52:14; Psalm 22:17).

Now because of the cross, we have a spiritual weapon as a CHAYIL army of God. The blood of Jesus prevailed against all evil and cried out for vengeance against Satanic forces for the cruelty suffered on the altar of God, the cross. Jesus Christ, EL CHAYIL, Lord of armies, King of glory, Lord of wealth wears His blood on His robe that cries out victory for all those who believe in the power of His cross: *"He is dressed in a robe dipped in **blood**, and his **name** is the **Word of God**. The armies of heaven were following him, riding on white horses and dressed in fine linen, white and clean"* (Revelation 19:13-14 emphasis added). Here we see three of God's spiritual weapons for spiritual warfare: the blood of Jesus, the name of Jesus, and the Word of God. These spiritual weapons have overcoming power.

> Then I heard a loud voice in heaven say: "Now have come the salvation and the power and the kingdom of our God, and the authority of his Christ. For the accuser of our brothers, who accuses them before our God day and night, has been hurled down. They overcame him by the blood of the Lamb and by the word of their testimony; they did not love their lives so much as to shrink from death" (Revelation 12:10-11).

For God our Father so loved the world that He gave permission to His Son Jesus to be the sacrificial Lamb on the altar of the cross, to be crucified for the sins of the world. For Jesus our Savior so loved the world that He voluntarily gave up Himself to die on the cross for *all* the sins, failures, mistakes, shame, guilt, and suffering of the world. For the Holy Spirit of God so loved the world that He held back all the angels who would have rescued their God from the cruelty of humanity, and gave Him the power of the Holy Spirit to fulfill His purpose, and with a cry of victory said, "It is finished" and gave up His spirit and died.

The Altar of God

Even in His death, the almighty power of Jesus Christ, EL CHAYIL, was demonstrated. The power of the Holy Spirit came upon Him after He was bleeding for hours on the cross, the human altar of sacrifice: *"And when Jesus had cried out again in a loud voice, he gave up his spirit."* (God the Father and God the Holy Spirit was actively engaged in the passion of the cross.) *"At that moment the curtain of the temple was torn in two from top to bottom. The earth shook and the rocks split."* (So powerful was His death that the veil of the temple that separated the holy from the most holy place was ripped in two from top to bottom, obviously not by human hands. This symbolized that the separation between mankind and God, Jews and Gentiles was over. As *one* we now have access to the holy presence of the God of Abraham and David, our Messiah Jesus Christ. The rocks broke into pieces in wrath at the crimes of those who put the innocent man, Jesus, Son of God, to such a shameful, cruel, and torturous death.) *"The tombs broke open and the bodies of many holy people who had died were raised to life."* (The earth shook, convulsed, and vomited out bodies of saints who had died, symbolizing that Jesus in one blow conquered death and the grave and gave eternal life to all who believe in Him) (Matthew 27:50-52).

No wonder the angels in Heaven eternally are worshiping the Lamb who was slain:

> Then I looked and heard the voice of many angels, numbering thousands upon thousands, and ten thousand times ten thousand. They encircled the throne and the living creatures and the elders. In a loud voice they sang: "Worthy is the Lamb, who was slain, to receive power and wealth and wisdom and strength and honor and glory and praise!" Then I heard every creature in heaven and on earth and under the earth and on the sea, and all that is in them, singing: "To him who sits on the throne and to

the Lamb be praise and honor and glory and power, forever and ever!" (Revelation 5:11-14).

And we, too, will worship the Lamb of God who was slain at our altars to our King of glory.

At the **church altar**, we celebrate communion in celebration of the **great altar** of God, the cross of Calvary upon which Jesus, the Lamb of God, was the ultimate sacrifice for all the sins of the world. We worship Elohim, our God and infinite Creator, as God our Father, Son, and Holy Ghost was engaged in the altar of the cross. Our Heavenly Father in love for His world gave His only beloved Son, Jesus, to be slain on a cross for the sins of His world. Our Son of God, Jesus Christ, volunteered and chose to give His life in a cruel death because of His love for His world. Our Holy Spirit of God empowered to Jesus to destroy the works of the evil one and to the end held Him together so that in strength He could give His final war cry and give up His life triumphantly on the cross.

We thank our Heavenly Father for the power of His love as He continues to Father us in love. We thank Jesus Christ for the provision of His grace that set us free and keeps us free to serve Him and bring glory to His name. We thank our Holy Spirit for His passionate power and strength, manifesting CHAYIL glory in and through us that will fulfill **Mission INFUSION** until the whole earth is full of the glory of Jesus Christ. May God's kingdom come on earth as it is in Heaven. We agree and continue the declarations of the prophets and the angels: *"And the glory of the Lord will be revealed, and all mankind together will **see** it. For the mouth of the Lord has spoken"* (Isaiah 40:5 emphasis added). *"And they [angels] were calling to one another: 'Holy, holy, holy is the Lord Almighty; the whole earth is full of his glory'"* (Isaiah 6:3).

CHAPTER 10

Altars of Abraham

Was not our ancestor Abraham considered righteous for what he did when he offered his son Isaac on the altar? (James 2:21).

It is interesting that before Noah, Abraham, and the patriarchs built houses for themselves, they first built altars unto the Lord. Building altars to maintain a strong relationship with God was important for their establishment, security, and success in family and business.

Abraham, before he was called by God, lived with his family in Ur of the Chaldees, which is in modern Iraq. The practice of the religious people in that land at that time was to worship several gods, and so did Abraham and his father Terah. *"Joshua said to all the people, 'This is what the Lord, the God of Israel, says: "Long ago your forefathers, including Terah the father of Abraham and Nahor, lived beyond the River and worshiped other gods""* (Joshua 24:2).

The custom of building altars for worship and offerings was first seen in the beginning where Cain and Abel offered sacrifices to God. *"In the course of time Cain brought some of the fruits of the soil as an offering to the Lord. But Abel brought fat portions from some of the firstborn of his flock. The Lord looked with favor on Abel and his offering"* (Genesis 4:2-4). This shows that God appreciates man's effort to seek Him, worship him, and honor Him with offerings.

When God called Abraham, who was then called Abram, He told him to leave his country, his father's household (his legacy), and his family, except for his wife Sarah, and to go to a new land, with new faith in Yahweh for a great calling to be a blessing to all the people of the earth (Genesis 12:1-3). Abraham obeyed and continued to learn about Yahweh, the true and living God, by nurturing a close relationship with God through building altars unto the Lord.

In his praise to God before the priest Melchizedek, we see where Abraham had renounced his former gods, describing the Lord as the Most High (supreme) God: *"But Abram said to the king of Sodom, 'I have raised my hand to the Lord, God Most High, Creator of heaven and earth, and have taken an oath'"* (Genesis 14:22). The God whom Abraham worshiped eventually sent His Son as a seed through the flesh of Abraham to become Jesus, Savior of the world. The covenant promise given to Abraham at his calling was fulfilled: *"And all peoples on earth will be blessed through you"* (Genesis 12:3).

ABRAHAM'S PERSONAL ALTAR

"So Abram left, as the Lord had told him; and Lot went with him. Abram was seventy-five years old when he set out from Haran. From there he went on toward the hills east of Bethel and pitched his tent, with Bethel on the west and Ai on the east. There he built an altar to the Lord and called on the name of the Lord" (Genesis 12:4,8). The first altar that Abraham built unto the Lord was his **personal altar**. Often in families, one person is saved first and has to nurture their faith in God in spite of being surrounded with misunderstandings and doubts in other family members. God had called Abraham personally, and his wife at that time had personal struggles and was overwhelmed by the call and its promises.

At his personal altar, God would encourage Abraham and help him to grow in faith in spite of delays, treachery, and family issues. God reminded him of the covenant promise for his descendants and that Sarah's womb would be healed, as with God nothing is impossible. Not only would Abraham be a father, but he would be a father of nations. In one such communion with God, the Lord said, *"I will surely return to you about this time next year, and Sarah your wife will have a son"* (Genesis 18:10). Sarah was listening to her husband talking with God, and she laughed, doubting the promise:

> So Sarah laughed to herself as she thought, "After I am worn out and my master is old, will I now have this pleasure?" Then the Lord said to Abraham, "Why did Sarah laugh and say, 'Will I really have a child, now that I am old?' Is anything too hard for the Lord? I will return to you at the appointed time next year and Sarah will have a son" (Genesis 18:10-14).

Abraham at his personal altar kept his faith alive for his sake, for his wife's sake, and for the sake of his calling to be a father of nations. *"Believe in the Lord Jesus, and you will be saved—you and your household"* (Acts 16:31).

A personal altar is a place of consecration, meeting with God daily for cleansing, worship, teaching, and instruction, so that faith and favor with God is nurtured and maintained for a lasting legacy. Abraham and Sarah went through great trials that sometimes wore out his faith, but at his personal altar, God refreshed and restored Abraham's faith for his miracle. We see an example of God ministering to His servant Abraham during his personal altar:

> After this, the word of the Lord came to Abram in a vision: "Do not be afraid, Abram. I am your shield, your very great reward." But Abram said, "O Sovereign Lord, what can you give me since I remain childless and the one who will inherit my estate is Eliezer of Damascus?" And Abram said, "You have given me no children; so a servant in my household will be my

heir." Then the word of the Lord came to him: "This man will not be your heir, but a son coming from your own body will be your heir." He took him outside and said, "Look up at the heavens and count the stars—if indeed you can count them." Then he said to him, "So shall your offspring be." Abram believed the Lord, and he credited it to him as righteousness (Genesis 15:1-6).

A consistent life of faith is not easy. It is a battle. While waiting for the miracle, the birds of prey (doubt, unbelief, shame, discouragement, and fear) come to eat away your faith with an assignment for you to abort your miracle. However, God at your personal altar times will comfort you, hold you together, and minister to you until your faith is restored and you are once again in righteousness (right standing in God to receive your miracle). Your personal altar is your great privilege with God to meet with God in a secret place where you can share your doubts, fears, and thoughts in a safe place that is just for you with God. As the apple of His eye, He is committed to love you and care for you, holding you together for your ultimate potential of greatness in Him.

ABRAHAM'S FAMILY ALTAR

So Abram went up from Egypt to the Negev, with his wife and everything he had, and Lot went with him. Abram had become very wealthy in livestock and in silver and gold. From the Negev he went from place to place until he came to Bethel, to the place between Bethel and Ai where his tent had been earlier and where he had first built an altar. There Abram called on the name of the Lord (Genesis 13:1-4).

Abraham and his family built a strong business both in farming and commodities, and he continued in his relationship with God by building altars. The obvious blessing of God in his life was evident, and he maintained the practice of building an altar to *"call on the name of the Lord."*

We can see from the continued practice of Abraham's son and grandson that their **family altar** so impacted them that even after Abraham was no longer alive, building altars for communion with God remained important to them. Abraham's son Isaac also built altars to call on the name of the Lord: *"Isaac built an altar there and called on the name of the Lord. There he pitched his tent, and there his servants dug a well"* (Genesis 26:25). Abraham's grandson Jacob also built altars to call on the name of the Lord: *"There he [Jacob] built an altar, and he called the place El Bethel, because it was there that God revealed himself to him when he was fleeing from his brother"* (Genesis 35:7). They followed the practice of building altars as Abraham did. Abraham was the priest of the family and taught them how to pray, worship God, and access the throne of God for mercy and help in times of need.

ABRAHAM'S TERRITORIAL ALTAR

Territorial altars are also called **community altars**.

The Lord said to Abram after Lot had parted from him, "Lift up your eyes from where you are and look north and south, east and west. All the land that you **see** I will give to you and your offspring forever. I will make your offspring like the dust of the earth, so that if anyone could count the dust, then your offspring could be counted. Go, **walk** through the length and breadth of the land, for I am giving it to you." So Abram moved his tents and went to live near the great trees of Mamre at Hebron, where **he built an altar to the Lord** (Genesis 13:14-18 emphasis added).

God gave Abraham during his personal altar the strategy for possessing and establishing a territory or promise:

First, SEE the land. What you see will birth faith in your heart to conceive your dream and make it become a *faith seed*. When faith comes into a heart with a dream, it surrounds it to form a faith seed. Only when your dream becomes a seed can it bring forth the harvest of its reality. This is called the law of seed and harvest: *"As long as the earth endures, seedtime and harvest..."* (Genesis 8:22). What you can *see* becomes your faith seed for your harvest of miracles.

Second, WALK the land. God gave Joshua this strategy as well: *"I will give you every place where you set your foot, as I promised Moses"* (Joshua 1:3). Walking the land is more than just going for a stroll. Jesus explained the power of walking by faith to destroy opposition to your promises: *"I have given you authority to trample on snakes and scorpions and to overcome all the power of the enemy; nothing will harm you"* (Luke 10:19). Moses never walked the land of promises, and he never possessed it. To "walk the land" is to walk by faith, doing the warfare necessary to keep your faith alive and to destroy the plans of Satan to block your possession. Your "walk" is more than your steps, it is your confident commitment and conviction in your heart. *"You used to walk in these ways, in the life you once lived"* (Colossians 3:7). To walk the land is to create your dream with the end in mind so that God can bless it.

By building a territorial altar on the land, he established it for generations by establishing a spiritual beachhead for God to rule in that land and for his descendants to occupy that land forever. The land was sealed with access to the throne of God, the Most High, as a spiritual ladder for angels to ascend and descend.

In areas where altars are built unto demonic principalities, there is usually high engagement with demons, spread of occult practices, poverty, diseases, corruption, and violence. *"Blessed is the nation whose God is the Lord, the people he chose for his inheritance"* (Psalm 33:12). Who or whatever is worshiped at territorial or community altars creates the atmosphere and environment of that community. The battle in every territory is over worship. The battle is over what kind of altar will be established. Altars establish gates of rule, ownership, and dominion.

ABRAHAM'S ALTAR OF SACRIFICE

Abraham's **altar of sacrifice** was the place of dying to himself, his dream, and his calling and offering up his beloved son to God to prove his consistent love and worship of God. God has placed a great demand on us: *"Love the Lord your God with **all** your heart and with **all** your soul and with **all** your strength"* (Deuteronomy 6:5 emphasis added). This means that God must remain first place in priority above anything and anyone in our lives.

After Abraham's and Sarah's test of long-term barrenness, the inability of Sarah to bear a child, God's powerful promise became a reality and Sarah, at ninety years old, bore Isaac, the promised seed of Abraham. Imagine the love and closeness of father and son. To add to the dynamics of the circumstances, Abraham and Sarah decided to have a son by Hagar, Sarah's maid, doubting that Sarah would ever have a child. Ishmael was Abraham's first-born son. Love and devotion was strong with them both. Eventually, however, God came through for Sarah and her son Isaac was born.

In a family with two sons with two different women, the competition and complication rose to the level of potential treachery, and Sarah feared for the life of Isaac. Abraham had to give up his first-born son Ishmael with a broken heart to preserve the seed of promise, Isaac. With Isaac as his son of promise, God visited Abraham with a great test of his love and devotion to God with his whole heart. The test: was Isaac an idol to Abraham? Was his love for Isaac greater than his love for God? Is obedience still a priority to God's friend, Abraham? Sometimes when we pray for a long time for a blessing, the blessing can take first place in our heart.

"Then God said, 'Take your son, your only son, Isaac, whom you love, and go to the region of Moriah. Sacrifice him there as a burnt offering on one of the mountains I will tell you about'" (Genesis 22:2). This was Abraham's altar of sacrifice—to die to the love of this life (his son and his calling), love God in obedience, and worship God with his greatest treasure. In reading of the great test in Job's life, one wonders if this too was a challenge from Satan to test Abraham; or was God satisfying a kingdom legal requirement to prove that even as He would one day offer up His beloved Son Jesus Christ on an altar of sacrifice, there was also a man on earth who loved God with all his heart and would give up his son as an obedient sacrifice to God. Jesus became the Lamb of God that was slain on a cross: *"The next day John saw Jesus coming toward him and said, 'Look, the Lamb of God, who takes away the sin of the world!'"* (John 1:29). *"For God so loved the world that he gave his one and only Son, that whoever believes in him shall not perish but have eternal life"* (John 3:16).

Abraham died in his heart, and God lived in his heart. Abraham died to his flesh, and his flesh became the flesh through whom the Son of God would be born into the world: *"A record of the genealogy of Jesus Christ the son of David, the son of Abraham"* (Matthew 1:1).

> When they reached the place God had told him about, Abraham built an altar there and arranged the wood on it. He bound his son Isaac and laid him on the altar, on top of the wood. Then he reached out his

hand and took the knife to slay his son. But the angel of the Lord called out to him from heaven, "Abraham! Abraham!" "Here I am," he replied. "Do not lay a hand on the boy," he said. "Do not do anything to him. **Now I know that you fear God, because you have not withheld from me your son, your only son**" (Genesis 22:9-12 emphasis added).

Wow! Abraham passed the test, and God showed him a ram that was already caught in a thicket for Abraham to sacrifice for God. Abraham named that place Jehovah Jireh, the Lord will provide.

Jesus, son of David, son of Abraham—two men who gave up everything to satisfy the kingdom legal requirement for Jesus, Son of Man, to die for the sins of all mankind. Two men who practiced obvious devotion, sacrifice, and generosity to God at their place of altars. Their relationship with God was strong on earth, and Jesus named them in His lineage forever. Altars are powerful to access God for unlimited glory, a prosperous life, and lasting legacy.

CHAPTER 11

Altar of Repentance

David built an altar to the Lord there and sacrificed burnt offerings and fellowship offerings. Then the Lord answered prayer in behalf of the land, and the plague on Israel was stopped (2 Samuel 24:25).

The Bible declares that sin has strong consequences: *"But now that you have been set free from sin and have become slaves to God, the benefit you reap leads to holiness, and the result is eternal life. For the wages of sin is death, but the gift of God is eternal life in Christ Jesus our Lord"* (Romans 6:22-23). Under the Old Covenant, the ark and altars were established to deal with the sins of people and to release the grace of God.

JOB'S ALTAR OF REPENTANCE

Job was a father of ten children. He was described as a righteous and God-fearing man. He was powerful, wealthy, and the priest of his home. As priest of his home, he watched over his family to ensure that they remained in right standing with God for His protection, peace, and continued favor. God favored Job's relationship with Him. *"In the land of Uz there lived a man whose name was Job. This man was blameless and upright; he feared God and shunned evil"* (Job 1:1).

Job's children, however, loved to party, and Job suspected that they were into excessive drinking. *"His sons used to take turns holding feasts in their homes, and they would invite their three sisters to eat and drink with them"* (Job 1:4). They were probably at the age where he could no longer dictate to them, but he would purposefully intercede for them and sacrificed burnt offerings for each child: *"When a period of feasting had run its course, Job would send and have them purified. Early in the morning he would sacrifice a burnt offering for each of them, thinking, 'Perhaps my children have sinned and cursed God in their hearts.' This was Job's regular custom"* (Job 1:5).

Daniel and Nehemiah repented for the sins of Israel and God had mercy. An **altar of repentance** can be personal, family, national, or anywhere the mercy of God is needed.

JACOB'S ALTAR OF REPENTANCE

Jacob was the grandson of Abraham. When Abraham was called by God, he built a territorial or community altar at Bethel. Now God was ready for Jacob to possess the land that He had promised to Abraham and His descendants.

> Then God said to Jacob, "Go up to Bethel and settle there, and **build an altar there to God**, who appeared to you when you were fleeing from your brother Esau." So Jacob said to his household and to all who were with him, "Get rid of the foreign gods you have with you, and purify yourselves and change your clothes. Then come, let us go up to Bethel, where I will build an altar to God, who answered me in the day of my distress and who has been with me wherever I have gone" (Genesis 35:1-3).

This is an example of a man cleansing his home of anything that was a reproach to God and ministering salvation and repentance to his family. His sons were worshiping

Altar of Repentance

foreign gods, forsaking the God of Abraham, Isaac, and Jacob. They were involved with cultural practices that were signs of paganism, such as wearing kinds of jewelry and clothes that were symbolic of foreign gods. They needed God to be with them and for them in their battle for establishment. God knew that temptation and sin started in the Garden of Eden with Satan successfully tempting and defiling them with evil. Now mankind has a malady; we are born in sin with a tendency toward sin.

In households were parents are saved, living in righteousness, Satan will always go after the children for generational control. Satan will never give up trying to bring people under his curse (away from the blessing of God). With this in mind, God's plan of salvation for the world includes His only Son, Jesus Christ, who died on a cross for the salvation of the world.

> For God so loved the world that he gave his one and only Son, that whoever believes in him shall not perish but have eternal life. For God did not send his Son into the world to condemn the world, but to save the world through him. Whoever believes in him is not condemned, but whoever does not believe stands condemned already because he has not believed in the name of God's one and only Son (John 3:16-19).

Jacob's family obeyed him, and an altar of repentance was built to the Lord, who shows mercy and keeps covenant. *"So they gave Jacob all the foreign gods they had and the rings in their ears, and Jacob buried them under the oak at Shechem. Then they set out, and the terror of God fell upon the towns all around them so that no one pursued them"* (Genesis 35:4,5). God's grace is greater than all sins, and His mercies are new every morning. They went to Bethel and built an altar of repentance, renewing their faith, reverence, and need of God. God's forgiveness and restoration resulted in their victory as they possessed the land that was promised to them.

Notice the power of altars: *"Then they set out, and the terror of God fell upon the towns all around them so that no one pursued them"* (Genesis 35:5). An altar is a gate or opened portal into the realm of the spirit for access to God's throne of glory. David prayed, *"Summon your power, O God; show us your strength, O God, as you have done before"* (Psalm 68:28). David wanted to see the manifested strength and power of God with His people. An altar to our King of glory establishes the government, kingdom, and rule of Jesus Christ in you, through you, and in the place it is built. An altar establishes a legal ground for the covenant blessings to flow to the ones who built it. It is a place of surrender to God to receive from God His glory, to glorify His name through you.

Surrender to receive power from God for release of power and manifested glory of Jesus Christ *in* and *through* you.

An altar for Jesus Christ is built by faith to intentionally establish His presence for His power, peace, mercy, government, and rule in that heart, place (home, school, work), or community.

DAVID'S ALTAR OF REPENTANCE

David had committed an act that grieved the Lord. The prophet came and told David that God was grieved and consequences of the sin were laid out. David was deeply sorrowful. *"David said to Gad, 'I am in deep distress. Let us fall into the hands of the Lord, for his mercy is great; but do not let me fall into the hands of men.' So the Lord sent a plague on Israel from that morning until the end of the time designated, and seventy thousand of the people from Dan to Beersheba died"* (2 Samuel 24:14-15). David repented and interceded and God sent again the Prophet Gad: *"On that day Gad went to David and said to him, '**Go up and build an altar to the Lord***

Altar of Repentance

on the threshing floor of Araunah the Jebusite'" (2 Samuel 24:18 emphasis added).

An **altar of repentance** with sacrificing animals as offerings to the Lord would satisfy the penalty of the sin of David by the shedding of blood. God had establish under the Old Covenant the sacrificial system—without the shedding of blood there would be no remission of sins. The blood sacrifice was the life of an innocent animal receiving death so that the one offering the sacrifice could go free. David obeyed God's direction: *"David built an altar to the Lord there and sacrificed burnt offerings and fellowship offerings. Then the Lord answered prayer in behalf of the land, and the plague on Israel was stopped"* (2 Samuel 24:25).

Through His death and resurrection, Christ took away our sins. *"The next day John saw Jesus coming toward him and said, 'Look, the Lamb of God, who takes away the sin of the world!'"* (John 1:29). The plague in our hearts and lives stops when we confess our sins and believe in our hearts that Jesus Christ is our Lord and Savior. *"For you know that it was not with perishable things such as silver or gold that you were redeemed from the empty way of life handed down to you from your forefathers, but with the precious blood of Christ, a lamb without blemish or defect"* (1 Peter 1:18-19). In our New Covenant with God, all who trust Jesus Christ as Savior become God's covenant people, His Church.

CHAPTER 12

Altar of Peace

So Gideon built an altar to the Lord there and called it The Lord is Peace (Judges 6:24).

The Hebrew word for *peace* is Shalom, and it is a powerful rich word like the word *CHAYIL*, with many meanings. It is so meaningful that to the Jews it is a greeting, a farewell, and a blessing. Shalom means completeness, soundness, health, prosperity, and peace. God's peace became a powerful delivering force for His people. Gideon and the Israelites were going through a very frustrating time with the marauding Midianite armies.

> Whenever the Israelites planted their crops, the Midianites, Amalekites and other eastern peoples invaded the country. They camped on the land and ruined the crops all the way to Gaza and did not spare a living thing for Israel, neither sheep nor cattle nor donkeys. They came up with their livestock and their tents like swarms of locusts. It was impossible to count the men and their camels; they invaded the land to ravage it. Midian so impoverished, the Israelites that they cried out to the Lord for help (Judges 6:3-6).

The word *impoverished* means reduced to poverty, bankrupted, deprived of strength and creativity, or experiencing severe loss.

The Midianite attack was a vicious attack that created cycles of loss. You work hard, and just before the harvest, the enemy comes in and steals all the harvest. With a recurrence of this, it can lead to frustration, discouragement, and depression. Gideon was obviously experiencing all that and more as he vented to God openly about the way he was feeling about himself and about God. Gideon was not a happy man, but he was a hard worker. *"The angel of the Lord came and sat down under the oak in Ophrah that belonged to Joash the Abiezrite, where his son Gideon was threshing wheat in a winepress to keep it from the Midianites. When the angel of the Lord appeared to Gideon, he said, 'The Lord is with you, mighty warrior'"* (Judges 6:11-12).

Gideon was strategically trying to beat the Midianites to reap and hide his harvest. He was not in a good mood for a visit from God or to be called "mighty warrior." This was not famine caused by lack of rain or natural disaster. This was suffering at the hand of vicious thieves. *"The thief comes only to steal and kill and destroy; I have come that they may have life, and have it to the full"* (John 10:10). This was a Satanic attack on the people of God.

The Lord, King of glory, mighty in battle, came down to *make* Gideon a mighty warrior. Through Gideon, He would empower and mobilize an army on earth to join His army in Heaven to destroy the Midianites and save Israel. When we go through long seasons of discouragement, faith, joy, peace, and courage can be diminished. God had to heal, restore, and prepare Gideon for his potential as a mighty warrior.

Gideon's preparation included:

1. **Restoration of relationship and faith in God.** Gideon vented his frustration with God, *"'But sir,' Gideon replied, 'if the Lord is with us, why has all this happened to us? Where are all his wonders that our fathers told us about when they said, "Did not the Lord bring us up out of Egypt?" But now the Lord has abandoned us and put us into the hand of Midian'"* (Judges 6:13). God restored

Altar of Peace

his faith by patiently listening and sharing until Gideon in restoration built an altar of peace with God. His altar of peace was a symbol.

a. **He had made peace *with* God.** He had forgiven God, and God had forgiven him. He was now in right relationship with God with access to the King of glory. Jesus Christ is called the Prince (Owner) of Peace. When we believe in Jesus as our Savior, our sins are forgiven and we have peace with God that our sins are no longer marked against us. *"God made him [Jesus] who had no sin to be sin for us, so that in him we might become the righteousness of God"* (2 Corinthians 5:21). As believers in Jesus Christ, we have peace with God.

b. **He had the peace *of* God.** God would empower him to become a mighty warrior. *"The Lord turned to him and said, 'Go in the strength you have and save Israel out of Midian's hand. Am I not sending you?'"* (Judges 6:14). God empowered Gideon with the grace of CHAYIL (strength, power, influence, wisdom, and strategy) to attract and develop a mighty army as God's ground troops that would fight with the Lord's army of angels. Gideon was transformed from being a man in hiding to become the bold commander of the army of Israel.

c. **He had peace *for* God.** The peace given to Gideon was for the sake of God and for Israel. God, by His kingdom law, uses a human army to bring His mission of salvation, deliverance, peace, repentance, revival, and restoration through human believers. He uses prophets, priests, kings, and ordinary people like Gideon whom He empowers and glorifies for His cause. With CHAYIL influence, Gideon attracted a great army of men who volunteered to fight with him. God, however, wanted to ensure that He would receive the glory as Savior of Israel. *"The Lord said to Gideon, 'With the three hundred men that lapped I will save you and give the Midianites into your hands. Let all the other men go, each to his own place'"* (Judges 7:7). God downsized the army of Gideon as this battle was the Lord's. By faith Gideon built an altar and called it **altar of peace**.

2. **Healing of a poor self-image.** *"'But Lord,' Gideon asked, 'how can I save Israel? My clan is the weakest in Manasseh, and I am the least in my family'"* (Judges 6:15). The Lord gently coached and restored Gideon to have faith in God. God would never leave nor forsake him. God would not send him out to fight by himself. *"The Lord answered, 'I will be with you, and you will strike down all the Midianites together'"* (Judges 6:16). David said that God's gentleness made him great. God is gentle toward His servants as He gives them a calling that is impossible for them. *"Jesus looked at them and said, 'With man this is impossible, but with God all things are possible'"* (Matthew 19:26). As previously stated, one of the meanings of the Hebrew word for peace, "shalom," is "to prosper." God would prosper Gideon as he prospered David with his CHAYIL army and the prophecy of success: *"Then the Spirit came upon Amasai, chief of the thirty, and he said: 'We are yours, O David! We are with you, O son of Jesse! Success, success to you, and success to those who help you, for your God will help you'"* (1 Chronicles 12:18). The Hebrew word for *success* is the same word for *peace*, Shalom.

3. **Worship with offerings.** "Gideon replied, *'If now I have found favor in your eyes, give me a sign that it is really you talking to me. Please do not go away until I*

Altar of Peace

come back and bring my offering and set it before you'" (Judges 6:17-18). The Bible says that as long as the earth endures, there is one principle that will never fade, "seed time and harvest." Worship with offerings shows God our hearts to give for faith to receive. The principle of mutual giving and serving in all relationships stands also with God. A heart with the grace of giving is a heart of gratefulness, and our offerings are seeds of gratitude as God's servants in His purpose and kingdom plans. Gideon recognized that although he was desperately storing harvest for his family, his offering to God would release him from lack to abundance and from frustration to become God's famous warrior. *"But the Lord said to him, 'Peace! Do not be afraid. You are not going to die.' So Gideon built an altar to the Lord there and called it The Lord is Peace. To this day it stands in Ophrah of the Abiezrites"* (Judges 6:23-24). God's declaration to Gideon of peace was received by Gideon, and He sealed it with an altar of peace.

Now for us, our hearts must be an altar of peace. In relationship with God, we worship Him in spirit and in truth, intentionally letting the peace of God rule our hearts. With our hearts as altars of peace, peace will guard our hearts and guide our ways into its paths of prosperity: *"And the peace of God, which transcends all understanding, will guard your hearts and your minds in Christ Jesus"* (Philippians 4:7). Our hearts must not be ruled by fear but by faith, not by confusion but by peace, not by hate but by love, and not by vain imaginations but by power. *"And the peace of God, which transcends all understanding, will guard your hearts and your minds in Christ Jesus"* (Philippians 4:7).

In addition to building an altar of peace, God instructed Gideon to destroy the national altar that was built on a high place by his father for worship to Baal:

That same night the Lord said to him, "Take the second bull from your father's herd, the one seven years old. Tear down your father's altar to Baal and cut down the Asherah pole beside it. Then build a proper kind of altar to the Lord your God on the top of this height. Using the wood of the Asherah pole that you cut down, offer the second bull as a burnt offering" (Judges 6:25-26).

This shows that for God's peace to reign in our lives, we have to get rid of anything that is offensive to God or displays allegiances to idols or Satan or spiritual practices that were not in the name of Jesus Christ.

Not only did Gideon had to destroy his father's altar to Baal, but he also had to cut down the Asherah pole beside it and burn it as fuel for a proper altar to the Lord God. God's altar must be on a high place for national worship and allegiance to the God of Gideon that would save them from the Midianites. God will not share His glory with demons or idols. This was not only a move of God to deliver Israel from the Midianites but also a move of reformation. The Israelites were practicing idolatry, the very reason why God had lifted His hand of protection and blessing from them. The altar of Baal today represents a false god, deceptive spiritual beliefs and activities, and tolerant practices that have become popular with disregard for God's opinion as stated clearly in the Bible.

As soon as the people heard throughout the community that the altar of Baal were destroyed and replaced by the altar of peace to Jehovah they became angry and wanted to kill Gideon:

> In the morning when the men of the town got up, there was Baal's altar, demolished, with the Asherah pole beside it cut down and the second bull sacrificed on the newly built altar! They asked each other, "Who did this?" When they carefully investigated, they were told, "Gideon son of Joash did it." The men of the town demanded of Joash, "Bring out your son. He must die,

Altar of Peace

because he has broken down Baal's altar and cut down the Asherah pole beside it" (Judges 6:28-30).

Israel, seed of Abraham, worshipers of Jehovah, had gone so far away from God that they were willing to defend Baal worship and kill God's prophet and judge mediating to save them.

Gideon's father, however, who had built the altar to Baal in the first place, intervened with reformation of his own heart: *"But Joash replied to the hostile crowd around him, 'Are you going to plead Baal's cause? Are you trying to save him? Whoever fights for him shall be put to death by morning! If Baal really is a god, he can defend himself when someone breaks down his altar'"* (Judges 6:31). His mediation was brilliant. If they so believed in their god, why would he need man to fight for him? Let Baal kill Gideon to prove his own power: *"So that day they called Gideon 'Jerub-Baal,' saying, 'Let Baal contend with him,' because he broke down Baal's altar"* (Judges 6:32). This was a curse put on Gideon.

Building spiritual altars to our King of glory is powerful. Gideon's altar of peace was more powerful than the altar to Baal. The occult leaders couldn't curse Gideon because his altar of peace made him saved, safe, and protected by our Almighty God, King of glory. When a man's ways pleases the Lord, He will make his enemies serve him. Gideon was successful in battle and the people who wanted to previously kill him, eventually wanted to serve him.

> The Israelites said to Gideon, "Rule over us-you, your son and your grandson-because you have saved us out of the hand of Midian." But Gideon told them, "I will not rule over you, nor will my son rule over you. The Lord will rule over you." And he said, "I do have one request, that each of you give me an earring from your share of the plunder." (It was the custom of the Ishmaelites to wear gold earrings) (Judges 8:22-24).

Whom God blesses no man can curse. If God is for you, who can succeed with wicked plans against you? Jesus Christ is our Most High God and King of glory. When we build spiritual altars to our King of glory, Jesus is lifted high to draw all people unto Him and display His manifested CHAYIL glory in all the earth.

CHAPTER 13

Altar of Intercession

So Joshua fought the Amalekites as Moses had ordered, and Moses, Aaron and Hur went to the top of the hill (Exodus 17:10).

A ***spiritual altar for intercession*** is where two or three come together in a place of agreement with God and each other to mediate for others and to enforce God's kingdom and will on earth. Jesus taught us to pray, *"Your kingdom come, your will be done on earth as it is in heaven"* (Matthew 6:10). He continued to exhort His disciples on the power of intercession: *"From the days of John the Baptist until now, the kingdom of heaven has been forcefully advancing, and forceful men lay hold of it"* (Matthew 11:12). This is declaring that there are times when you have to be forceful against stubborn demons that come with an agenda to steal, kill, and destroy.

Jesus tells us how to build a spiritual altar of intercession:

> I tell you the truth, whatever you bind on earth will be bound in heaven, and whatever you loose on earth will be loosed in heaven. Again, I tell you that if two of you on earth agree about anything you ask for, it will be done for you by my Father in heaven. For where two or three come together in my name, there am I with them (Matthew 18:18-20).

BUILDING AN ALTAR OF INTERCESSION

1. ***Two or three come together in the name of Jesus.*** *"For where two or three come together in my name, there am I with them."* This is intentional communion with God for the purposes of God and to enforce God's kingdom to rule in situations that need the power of our Lord of glory. It is praying according to God's will and to neutralize opposition: *"This is the confidence we have in approaching God: that if we ask anything according to his will, he hears us. And if we know that he hears us—whatever we ask—we know that we have what we asked of him"* (1 John 5:14-15). EL CHAYIL is Lord of armies, King of glory, Lord of wealth and at a spiritual altar of intercession to our King of glory, you create an army that will be joined by the armies of Heaven to battle the kingdom of darkness. Jesus is our King of glory, strong and mighty, mighty in battle, our Lord Almighty.

David's psalm describes his revelation of EL CHAYIL: *"Who is this King of glory? The Lord strong and mighty, the Lord mighty in battle"* (Psalm 24:8). He worshiped God as King of glory and lived a life with great battles and great victories. David was a "kingdom enforcer," and he gave himself no rest until the covenant promise (God's will that Israel be a great nation) was a reality. When Israel came under attack by the Philistines, David became a solution: *"David asked the men standing near him, 'What will be done for the man who kills this Philistine and removes this disgrace from Israel? Who is this uncircumcised Philistine that he should defy the armies of the living God?'"* (1 Samuel 17:26). David was a volunteer in the armies of God, and

God promoted him as a leader in the army of Israel. David became famous as a mighty warrior like His God, and God promoted him as king of Israel.

2. ***Two or three come together in agreement.*** *"Again, I tell you that if two of you on earth agree about anything you ask for, it will be done for you by my Father in heaven."* In the place of intentional agreement for intentional results, the law of synergy kicks in and makes an altar of intercession powerful. Synergy can be described as the interaction of elements that create greater effect and release of power when combined in unity, versus the sum total of individual elements operating on their own. In other words, you praying by yourself will have less effect than praying with others. Praying by yourself is powerful, and praying with others in agreement creates cumulative power for even greater effect: *"How could one man chase a thousand, or two put ten thousand to flight, unless their Rock had sold them, unless the Lord had given them up?"* (Deuteronomy 32:30). The power of your intercession increases exponentially for greater manifested glory in corporate prayer of agreement.

In **corporate prayer**, the mindset and language must shift to declare an altar of intercession. Your manifestation and attitude will follow your declaration: *"Five of you will chase a hundred, and a hundred of you will chase ten thousand, and your enemies **will fall by the sword before you"*** (Leviticus 26:8 emphasis added). We have a powerful sword in our mouths like our Commander EL CHAYIL:

> The armies of heaven were following him, riding on white horses and dressed in fine linen, white and clean. Out of his mouth comes **a sharp sword** with which to strike down the nations.

"He will rule them with an iron scepter." He treads the winepress of the fury of the wrath of God Almighty. On his robe and on his thigh he has this name written: KING OF KINGS AND LORD OF LORDS (Revelation 19:13-16 emphasis added).

As His army of intercession, you have His sword in your mouth, the Word of the Lord, which is called the sword of the Spirit: *"Take the helmet of salvation and the sword of the Spirit, which is the word of God"* (Ephesians 6:17).

When you come in agreement at a spiritual altar of intercession, you pray, fight in spiritual warfare, and make your declarations for yourself, your health, your family, your finances, your church, your nation, etc. according to God's Word. When the enemy blocks your prayers, he is undermining God's Word and negating the power of our Lord Jesus Christ. That is why you are called a "kingdom enforcer," that is, forcefully advancing against opposition to the integrity of God's promises.

3. ***Together with authority.*** *"I tell you the truth, whatever you bind on earth will be bound in heaven, and whatever you loose on earth will be loosed in heaven."* All authority was given to Jesus to distribute to His army of kingdom enforcers. Among the many meanings of the Hebrew word CHAYIL are power, strength, elite forces, special forces, trained, equipped, and army. The cross was a victorious battle for Jesus, who won back for His believers the power, authority, and glory that they lost in the Garden of Eden. Before His ascension, He said to His disciples, *"All authority in heaven and on earth has been given to me. Therefore go and make disciples of all nations, baptizing them in the name of the Father and of the Son and of the Holy*

Spirit, and teaching them to obey everything I have commanded you. And surely I am with you always, to the very end of the age" (Matthew 28:18-20). Jesus is training a powerful CHAYIL army of elite forces that is trained with spiritual weapons, tactical strategies like altars to our King of glory, with CHAYIL force to forcefully advance the kingdom of our King.

Not only do we have the authority of Jesus, but we also have His power: *"But you will receive **power** when the Holy Spirit comes on you; and you will be my **witnesses** in Jerusalem, and in all Judea and Samaria, and to the ends of the earth"* (Acts 1:8 emphasis added). You have the power to manifest His glory as a witness that Jesus is alive and working through His servants. CHAYIL glory is the manifested power and glory of the Lord Jesus Christ in and through His servants. Your testimony will prove that your God is greater.

4. **Together in unity.** *"For where two or three come together in my name, there am I with them."* Unity is a powerful force: *"The Lord said, 'If as one people speaking the same language they have begun to do this, then nothing they plan to do will be impossible for them'"* (Genesis 11:6). Declarations during the altar of intercession are powerful. What you decree is established. What you declare, God will create. The ultimate secret is this: "You are made in the image of God to speak like God words of faith to create and rule your world." As you intercede with the same intention and result and in agreement with God's will, all things become possible: *"But with one accord they too had broken off the yoke and torn off the bonds"* (Jeremiah 5:5).

MOSES' ALTAR OF INTERCESSION

Moses created a spiritual altar of intercession with a spiritual army of three. *"The Amalekites came and attacked the Israelites at Rephidim. Moses said to Joshua, 'Choose some of our men and go out to fight the Amalekites. Tomorrow I will stand on top of the hill with the staff of God in my hands'"* (Exodus 17:8-9). Moses knew that God, I AM that I AM, was Lord of armies. Joshua mobilized his army as Moses instructed. Moses mobilized his army:

> So Joshua fought the Amalekites as Moses had ordered, and Moses, Aaron and Hur went to the top of the hill. As long as Moses held up his hands, the Israelites were winning, but whenever he lowered his hands, the Amalekites were winning. When Moses' hands grew tired, they took a stone and put it under him and he sat on it. Aaron and Hur held his hands up—one on one side, one on the other—so that his hands remained steady till sunset. So Joshua overcame the Amalekite army with the sword (Exodus 17:10-13).

Joshua won the battle by physical swords, Moses won the battle by spiritual weapons in his altar of intercession, and EL CHAYIL, Lord of armies, King of glory, fought with and for them. *"For the Lord your God is the one who goes with you to fight for you against your enemies to give you victory"* (Deuteronomy 20:4).

MOSES' ALTAR OF VICTORY

Moses exalted God by building an **altar of victory**: *"Moses built an altar and called it The Lord is my Banner. He said, "For hands were lifted up to the throne of the Lord. The Lord will be at war against the Amalekites from generation to* *generation"* (Exodus 17:15-16). Moses gave God the glory for the victory, acknowledging the power of his altar of intercession—"Hands lifted up to the throne of the Lord"—that the armies of God were engaged to fight with and for them. When God is engaged in your battle, His banner of victory is lifted high as He intercedes with you and commands the battle.

In our altar of intercession, Jesus joins in our intercession. When we come together in His name, He is there in our midst to command our prayer, declarations, and strategic actions: *"Who is he that condemns? Christ Jesus, who died—more than that, who was raised to life—is at the right hand of God and is also interceding for us"* (Romans 8:34). He comes with an army of His angels to guarantee our victory: *"But thanks be to God! He gives us the victory through our Lord Jesus Christ"* (1 Corinthians 15:57). Jesus Christ is David's King of glory who is mighty in battle. An altar of intercession is powerful with Jesus Christ leading and commanding as EL CHAYIL, Lord of armies, King of glory, Lord of wealth.

CHAPTER 14

Divine Interventions

> Oh, that you would rend the heavens and come down, that the mountains would tremble before you! (Isaiah 64:1).

There are world events that trigger a move of God, divine visitations, and divine interventions throughout the ages. When enough is enough, God comes down with an aggressive plan for salvation and restoration that includes spiritual and natural tactics.

The prophet Isaiah prayed that God would come down for divine intervention:

> Oh, that you would rend the heavens and **come down**, that the mountains would tremble before you! As when fire sets twigs ablaze and causes water to boil, **come down to make your name known to your enemies and cause the nations to quake before you**! For when you did awesome things that we did not expect, **you came down**, and the mountains trembled before you. Since ancient times no one has heard, no ear has perceived, no eye has seen any God besides you, who acts on behalf of those who wait for him (Isaiah 64:1-4 emphasis added).

This cry from the prophet Isaiah came at a time when Israel was in desperation as a nation, a religion, and land. The temple was burnt down, the city was desolate, the land was no longer flourishing as before, the people were ravished, and many were carried into captivity to a land far away. In addition, the people's hearts were far from God, with a focus on materialism versus reverence for God. They had forgotten the God who prospered them. The nation was in crisis, and their only hope was to look to a Higher Power that was greater than their own military power. They needed the Lord God of Israel to come down to their rescue, reformation, and redevelopment. They needed a fresh move of God, a revival, a restoration of truth and proper focus. It was time for divine intervention.

Now our world is rapidly spinning into a crisis. What was a cold war is now a global, open, and hostile war without borders. All nations are at risk. People are not safe in the air, land, or sea. Planes are exploding in the air or being shot down at random; bomb explosions happen anywhere; hostile religiously motivated wars are becoming more brutal; uncontrollable terrorism is becoming more and more intimidating and no one in any religion is safe; super powers are aligning for world domination; and outbreaks of epidemics can quickly become pandemics because of land, air, and sea travel.

Nature is showing its furious power in reaction to man-made environmental pollution (its cause and effects); nations are experiencing unprecedented natural disasters of floods, raging fires, tornadoes, ice storms, hurricanes, volcanic eruptions, earthquakes, tsunamis, and other ecological disasters. Nature is showing its uncontrollable power so that mankind will recognize that there are greater powers than manpower and be humbled to seek our God and Creator.

Humanitarian crises are increasing as millions of people in many nations are displaced, living in exile with great risk, in poverty and in suffering. There are over one billion people living in abject poverty without basic needs for survival. Aid and relief organizations cannot keep up with natural and war disasters. Poverty is a vice of evil that is keeping people subdued and powerless to dream and to believe for a better tomorrow.

Super powers are trying to figure out a new form of world governance for world preservation. Currently there is no worldwide military, legislature, rules of engagement, or constitution with jurisdiction over the entire planet. Nations are increasing their military power, and in a world with hunger crises, money is being spent on more military power because of fear, greed, and power struggles. Weapons of mass destruction are in the hands of unstable political figures.

The economy and economic disasters of one nation can have global effects on the world economy because of speculative bubbles and crashes. This was seen in the years from 2007 to 2012 when America's banking and housing crisis had global effects. Billionaires like Warren Buffet and Donald Trump are openly sharing their concerns for the American economy and other impending crises. It is time for divine intervention.

The Bible teaches that natural warfare is triggered by spiritual warfare. The real war is not people against people but is the continuation of an old war of Satan against humanity: *"For we do not wrestle against flesh and blood, but against principalities, against powers, against the rulers of the darkness of this age, against spiritual hosts of wickedness in the heavenly places"* (Ephesians 6:12 NKJV). Our world is now under siege by a conglomerate of seven evil principalities: pride, corruption, violence, perversion, occultism, deception, and poverty. It is a Leviathan attack.

The Bible talks about Leviathan, a snake with many heads: *"But you, O God, are my king from of old; you bring salvation upon the earth. It was you who split open the sea by your power; you broke the heads of the monster in the waters. It was you who crushed the heads of Leviathan and gave him as food to the creatures of the desert"* (Psalm 74:12-14). The chief commander of the Leviathan attack is Satan, otherwise called the devil: *"Therefore rejoice, you heavens and you who dwell in them! But woe to the earth and the sea, because the devil has gone down to you! He is filled with fury, because he knows that his time is short"* (Revelation 12:12).

When the world would reach a tipping point of evil, destruction, and potential implosion, God would come down throughout generations for visitation and divine intervention in the affairs of the world. These visitations can be called a move of God (with activity and manifestation of the Holy Spirit), a revival, an awakening, restoration of truth, or a refreshing. People are praying and hearts of believers are stirring as the Church is being prepared to take the center stage for a new move of God. Each time God comes down, He releases power and great glory in a person or a team to fulfill His mission for that season.

IN THE DAYS OF NOAH, GOD CAME DOWN

In the days of Noah, God came down to cleanse the world of evil and to save a remnant for re-development.

> Now the earth was corrupt in God's sight and was full of **violence**. God saw how **corrupt** the earth had become, for all the people on earth had corrupted their ways. So God said to Noah, "I am going to put an end to all people, for the earth is filled with violence because of them. I am surely going to destroy both them and the earth. So make yourself an ark of cypress wood" (Genesis 6:11-14 emphasis added).

When violence and corruption reaches a tipping point that is triggering the infusion of evil in kingdoms, societies, and people, God comes down with a cleansing and restoration plan.

God came down, and after conversations with Noah, He empowered him with CHAYIL glory (power, ability, strength, creativity, expertise, excellence, efficiency, and endurance) to build an ark that was greater than the ship *Titanic,* at a time when he had never experienced rain, much less a flood. This was not just to be a natural accomplishment but the result of man working with the CHAYIL glory of God to fulfill God's purpose on earth. There was a need for drastic measures for cleansing the world, preserving humanity, and fulfilling God's ultimate plan.

God manifested His power, glory, and sovereign rule by cleansing the earth by flood and saving Noah and His family to begin to create a new world. Unfortunately, while Noah and his family were saved physically, with contaminated hearts they started a new cycle of sin; they reproduced and developed a world that continues with cycles of increased corruption and oppression, as we are experiencing today.

IN THE DAYS OF MOSES, GOD CAME DOWN

God came down to His servant Moses for a visitation, divine intervention, and salvation of the Israelites from slavery, oppression, and mass murders.

> The Lord said, "I have indeed seen the misery of my people in Egypt. I have heard them crying out because of their slave drivers, and I am concerned about their suffering. So I have come down to rescue them from the hand of the Egyptians and to bring them up out of that land into a good and spacious land, a land flowing with milk and honey—the home of the Canaanites, Hittites, Amorites, Perizzites, Hivites and Jebusites. And now the cry of the Israelites has reached me, and I have seen the way the Egyptians are oppressing them. So now, go. I am sending you to Pharaoh to bring my people the Israelites out of Egypt" (Exodus 3:7-10).

It was time for salvation, and it was harvest time. God empowered Moses with the CHAYIL glory of the Great I AM, and God gained glory in Egypt and in the surrounding nations. Now the movie, *The Ten Commandments*, still brings glory to God and displays the power and glory of God through His servant Moses.

CHAYIL glory, unlike Shekinah glory, is the manifested glory of God working in and through His servant. The word *Shekinah* does not appear in the Bible, but the view does. The Jewish rabbis used this word, a form of a Hebrew word that means "He caused to dwell or inhabit." Shekinah describes the manifested presence of God with the people of God, as seen with the Israelites as they travelled through the wilderness: *"He guided them with the cloud by day and with light from the fire all night"* (Psalm 78:14). Whenever the people saw the cloud and fire in the sky, they knew that God's Shekinah glory was with them. It was a divine visitation of the manifested presence or dwelling of Jehovah God on the earth.

God's Shekinah glory was also seen and experienced in Solomon's temple: *"When the priests withdrew from the Holy Place, the cloud filled the temple of the Lord. And the priests could not perform their service because of the cloud, for the [shekinah] glory of the Lord filled his temple"* (1 Kings 8:10-11). Shekinah glory is the manifested glory of God around people as evidence of His presence.

CHAYIL glory, however, is the manifested power and glory of God *in* and *through* His servants: *"Then the Lord said to Moses, 'See, **I have made you like God to Pharaoh**, and your brother Aaron will be your prophet'"* (Exodus 7:1 emphasis added). God empowered Moses with CHAYIL glory to destroy the oppressive forces of His people. Moses would speak like God, and signs and wonders followed. Moses made declarations to Pharaoh about plagues in Egypt when he stubbornly refused to let God's people go, and God performed what Moses declared.

CHAYIL is a rich Hebrew word with many meanings, and according to *Strong's Concordance*, its three main meanings are power, army, and wealth. With Moses empowered with the CHAYIL glory of God, the salvation plan of God for His people included restoration of harvest. It was harvest time! It was payback time! God's salvation plan included the harvest of people, land, and resources. The word *salvation* is a holistic word that means rescue, restoration, well-being, prosperity, favor, and peace. When God came down with a mission to save His people from the slavery, oppression, and violence in Egypt, His harvest was loosed in three areas: people, land, and resources.

Now a new move of God, the CHAYIL Glory Movement, is causing ordinary believers to be filled with the power and glory of our Lord Jesus Christ (to flow *in* and *through* them) as He did through men and women of faith in the Bible and in previous moves of God on earth. In this outpouring of God's glory, His harvest will be loosed and reaped in three areas: harvest of souls, land, and resources. *"Therefore God exalted him to the highest place and gave him the name that is above every name, that at the name of Jesus every knee should bow, in heaven and on earth and under the earth, and every tongue confess that Jesus Christ is Lord, to the glory of God the Father"* (Philippians 2:9-11). It is a movement of transformation of lives, communities, and nations.

As in the days of Moses, harvest is being released in people, land, and resources:

1. **Harvest of people.** *"Then the Lord said to Moses, 'Go to Pharaoh and say to him, "This is what the Lord says: Let my people go, so that they may worship me"'"* (Exodus 8:1). True salvation is freedom to worship the one and only true God, Jehovah, and His Son, Jesus Christ. God is jealous for His worship and wants all people to worship Him alone. Salvation means that Jesus is not only Savior but Savior and Lord, with the hearts of His sons and daughters as altars for His glory.

2. **Harvest of land.** *"So I have come down to rescue them from the hand of the Egyptians and to bring them up out of that land into a good and spacious*

land, *a land flowing with milk and honey—the home of the Canaanites, Hittites, Amorites, Perizzites, Hivites and Jebusites"* (Exodus 3:8). The lands for God's people were specifically chosen, but they were occupied. God would infuse His CHAYIL army of Israelites with His power and glory to possess and occupy lands and to establish Israel as a great nation. Joshua, David, and their CHAYIL armies conquered all the land that God had promised them.

3. ***Harvest of resources.*** *"And I will make the Egyptians favorably disposed toward this people, so that when you leave you will not go empty-handed. Every woman is to ask her neighbor and any woman living in her house for articles of silver and gold and for clothing, which you will put on your sons and daughters. And so you will plunder the Egyptians"* (Exodus 3:21-22). It was payback time for the Israelites. They were sons of Abraham, Isaac, and Jacob, and therefore covenant wealth was their inheritance.

When Jacob and his family came to Egypt, Joseph, his son, was the chief of staff to the pharaoh of Egypt and the main cause of the economic prosperity of Egypt during a time of severe famine. Jacob and his sons, including Joseph, had wealthy families. The kingdom of Egypt, however, after the death of several pharaohs and Joseph, not only stole their wealth but subdued them into slavery, oppression, and violent torment.

God gave Moses the strategy how to loose and reap the harvest as His mission was not only salvation but the restoration of resources stolen for hundreds of years with compound interest. *"The Israelites did as Moses instructed and asked the Egyptians for articles of silver and gold and for clothing. The Lord had made the Egyptians favorably disposed toward the people, and they gave them what they asked for; so they plundered the Egyptians"* (Exodus 12:35-36).

Notice the people had to be engaged in reaping the harvest. In this CHAYIL Glory Movement, your ears will be cleared to *hear* instructions and your eyes cleared to *see* opportunities. *El Roi* is God who sees and causes His servants to see the opportunities provided by Him as manifested glory.

IN THE DAYS OF JOSHUA, GOD CAME DOWN

God came down to His servant Joshua for a visitation, divine intervention, and a mission to help the Israelites to possess their promised land in spite of all opposing forces. As Moses' successor, he was to complete the work that his great leader had begun.

> Now when Joshua was near Jericho, he looked up and saw a man standing in front of him with a drawn sword in his hand. Joshua went up to him and asked, "Are you for us or for our enemies?" "Neither," he replied, "but as commander of the army of the Lord I have now come." Then Joshua fell face down to the ground in reverence, and asked him, "What message does my Lord have for his servant?" The commander of the Lord's army replied, "Take off your sandals, for the place where you are standing is holy." And Joshua did so (Joshua 5:13-15).

EL CHAYIL is Lord of armies, King of glory, Lord of wealth. God came down and named Himself according to His agenda for manifested CHAYIL glory. He was commander of the army of the Lord, who had come down to train and mobilize a mighty army on earth to join with His angelic host of mighty warriors. His people were in a wilderness for forty years and too weak to advance and possess their promise. It was a time for visitation, divine intervention, and to loose His harvest of land and resources. He empowered His servant Joshua with CHAYIL glory (power, strength, might, wisdom, strategy, and influence) to go forward with a passionate mobilized army to possess and occupy their promised lands. God was with them. EL CHAYIL, Lord of armies, would empower Joshua to mobilize an Israelite army to join the armies of the Lord for battle against forces opposing Israel's establishment.

Joshua became a CHAYIL general with power and glory to fight in God's mighty army. He was successful in many military campaigns and possessed the lands designated by God for the Israelites.

> So Joshua subdued the whole region, including the hill country, the Negev, the western foothills and the mountain slopes, together with all their kings. He left no survivors. He totally destroyed all who breathed, just as the Lord, the God of Israel, had commanded. Joshua subdued them from Kadesh Barnea to Gaza and from the whole region of Goshen to Gibeon. All these kings and their lands Joshua conquered in one campaign, because the Lord, the God of Israel, fought for Israel (Joshua 10:40-42).

When God comes down, the impossible before becomes possible; the unreachable becomes reachable; and dreams become a reality. He comes down with His CHAYIL elite forces of angels to join us in our battles and release in us fresh power and glory for salvation, victories, and restoration: *"For the Lord your God is the one who goes with you to fight for you against your enemies to give you victory"* (Deuteronomy 20:4).

Joshua supervised with great CHAYIL wisdom and power the division of the conquered land and territories among the twelve tribes of Israel. Most of all, he ministered to the people to keep their hearts right and in strong covenant with God for continued blessings and favor. His name, Joshua, means "the Lord is salvation," and his life demonstrated the CHAYIL glory of the Lord that manifested in great power, victories, and salvation. God was the Savior, and Joshua was His servant of salvation.

IN THE DAYS OF GIDEON, GOD CAME DOWN

God came down to a frustrated and bankrupt man called Gideon and declared him a "mighty warrior."

> The angel of the Lord came and sat down under the oak in Ophrah that belonged to Joash the Abiezrite, where his son Gideon was threshing wheat in a winepress to keep it from the Midianites. When the angel of the Lord appeared to Gideon, he said, "The Lord is with you, mighty warrior" (Judges 6:11-12).

In this CHAYIL Glory Movement, God is using ordinary people whose weaknesses will be turned to strength so that the name of Jesus Christ will gain glory to the glory of our Father. God made sure that it would be known and seen that Israel was not saved by a person (man power) or by an army (military power) but by God for His glory.

> The Lord said to Gideon, "You have too many men for me to deliver Midian into their hands. In order that Israel may not boast against me that her own strength has saved her, announce now to the people, 'Anyone who trembles with fear may turn back and leave Mount Gilead.'" So twenty-two thousand men left, while ten thousand remained (Judges 7:2-3).

God was still not satisfied and asked Gideon to downsize his army until only three hundred men were left: *"The Lord said to Gideon, 'With the three hundred men that lapped,* **I will save you and give the Midianites into your**

hands. *Let all the other men go, each to his own place'"* (Judges 7:7 emphasis added). God's glory would be seen through Gideon and his small army. CHAYIL glory is the manifested power and glory of the Lord Jesus Christ *in* and *through* His servants.

Gideon prospered as a mighty leader of Israel, as their commander in successful military campaigns. He was careful in managing his fame with wisdom and honor: *"The Israelites said to Gideon, 'Rule over us—you, your son and your grandson—because you have saved us out of the hand of Midian.' But Gideon told them, 'I will not rule over you, nor will my son rule over you. The Lord will rule over you'"* (Judges 8:22-23).

CHAYIL glory is covenant glory that goes back to God. God glorifies His servants so that they can bring Him glory multiplied and make His name famous. When people hear and see His glory, they will give Him glory and spread His glory everywhere through testimonies. God blessed His servant Gideon with great victories, glory, and resources, and the land enjoyed peace during his lifetime: *"Thus Midian was subdued before the Israelites and did not raise its head again. During Gideon's lifetime, the land enjoyed peace forty years"* (Judges 8:28).

IN THE DAYS OF DAVID, GOD CAME DOWN

Israel and the Philistines were at war, a war that continued throughout the lifetime of King Saul, its ruler. This time, the Philistines chose a man-to-man combat between an Israelite soldier and a Philistine giant called Goliath.

> A champion named Goliath, who was from Gath, came out of the Philistine camp. He was over nine feet tall. He had a bronze helmet on his head and wore a coat of scale armor of bronze weighing five thousand shekels; on his

Divine Intervention

legs he wore bronze greaves, and a bronze javelin was slung on his back. His spear shaft was like a weaver's rod, and its iron point weighed six hundred shekels. His shield bearer went ahead of him. Goliath stood and shouted to the ranks of Israel, "Why do you come out and line up for battle? Am I not a Philistine, and are you not the servants of Saul? Choose a man and have him come down to me. If he is able to fight and kill me, we will become your subjects; but if I overcome him and kill him, you will become our subjects and serve us." Then the Philistine said, "This day I defy the ranks of Israel! Give me a man and let us fight each other." On hearing the Philistine's words, Saul and all the Israelites were dismayed and terrified (1 Samuel 17:4-11).

The great King Saul and the entire Israelite army were paralyzed by one man. It was time for divine intervention.

Goliath was a mighty man not only with great physical power but, as in modern-day wrestling, he also was skillful in using intimidation strategies with theatrics and shouting. He looked powerful, he shouted curses, and he inspired paralyzing fear that destabilized King Saul. Goliath also used occult power to release curses as flaming arrows that imploded in the ears of their hearers. What the people heard, believed and received, they became—fearful and weak opponents.

Goliath tried to intimidate and curse David by his gods:

Meanwhile, the Philistine, with his shield bearer in front of him, kept coming closer to David. He looked David over and saw that he was only a boy, ruddy and handsome, and he despised him. He said to David, "Am I a dog that you come at me with sticks?" And the Philistine cursed David by his gods. "Come here," he said, "and I'll give your flesh to the birds of the air and the beasts of the field!" (1 Samuel 17:41-44).

It became a battle of gods and words before it became a battle of physical weapons:

David said to the Philistine, "You come against me with sword and spear and javelin, but I come against you in the name of the Lord Almighty, the God of the armies of Israel, whom you have defied. This day the Lord will hand you over to me, and I'll strike you down and cut off your head. Today I will give the carcasses of the Philistine army to the birds of the air and the beasts of the earth, and the whole world will know that there is a God in Israel" (1 Samuel 17:45-47).

God would gain glory in many nations because of His servant David. God was the Savior, and David would be His servant of salvation.

What David was bold enough to declare, God performed. God *"carries out the words of his servants and fulfills the predictions of his messengers"* (Isaiah 44:26). *"Then the Lord said to me, 'You have seen well, for I am ready to perform My word'"* (Jeremiah 1:12 NKJV). Goliath was killed by David and his head chopped off by his own sword, just as David declared. God gained great glory through His servant David: *"All those gathered here will know that it is not by sword or spear that the Lord saves; for the battle is the Lord's, and he will give all of you into our hands"* (1 Samuel 17:47). God was the Savior of Israel, and David was His servant of salvation.

It is now time for visitation, divine intervention, and salvation in our day as the world groans for salvation and deliverance. Jesus has come down with His CHAYIL glory for such a time when our world is in crisis, crippling fear is being released upon nations, and there is no safe place except protection from God. Jesus spoke of a time of His visitation with CHAYIL glory:

> "There will be signs in the sun, moon and stars. On the earth, nations will be in anguish and perplexity at the roaring and tossing of the sea. Men will faint from terror, apprehensive of what is coming on the world, for the heavenly bodies will be shaken. At that time they will see the **Son of Man** coming in a cloud with

power and great glory [CHAYIL glory]. When these things begin to take place, stand up and lift up your heads, because your redemption is drawing near" (Luke 21:25-28 emphasis added).

It is time for His manifested CHAYIL glory in the earth. The Lord Jesus Christ will be the Hiding Place for His believers and will show forth His glory in and through them as promised: *"And all mankind will see God's salvation"* (Luke 3:6). *"And the glory of the Lord will be revealed, and all mankind together will see it. For the mouth of the Lord has spoken"* (Isaiah 40:5). We must give God permission to fill us afresh with His power and glory. Jesus Christ is the Savior of our world, and His Christian believers shall be His servants of salvation.

We will pray like David, *"Be exalted, O God, above the heavens; let your glory be over all the earth"* (Psalm 57:11). Jesus is the Savior of the world, and we are His servants of salvation. CHAYIL glory is the manifested power and glory of the Lord Jesus Christ *in* and *through* His servants.

Get ready for the outpouring of fresh power and great glory: *"Through the victories you gave [David] his glory is great; you have bestowed on him splendor and majesty"* (Psalm 21:5). David received power and great glory to serve God and to bring glory to His name. Through David, God triggered a move of God with a mission to destroy the enemies of Israel and to establish Israel as a strong a powerful nation. Now us.

Mission INFUSION is to *infuse* the CHAYIL glory of the Lord Jesus Christ in every heart, home, community, and nation. *"And they were calling to one another: 'Holy, holy, holy is the Lord Almighty; the whole earth is full of his glory'"* (Isaiah 6:3). Jesus Christ is the Savior and Hope of our world.

CHAPTER 15

Mission INFUSION

For the earth will be filled with the knowledge of the glory of the Lord, as the waters cover the sea (Habakkuk 2:14).

Mission INFUSION is to *infuse* the CHAYIL glory of the Lord Jesus Christ in every heart, home, community, and nation. It is called CHAYIL glory because of its intention and effect. CHAYIL glory means powerful, kinetic, active, strategic, moving, and manifesting glory in and through believing servants. Christ, our Hope of glory, can be dormant glory in Christians—not seen, shown, or heard. Jesus understood this principle: *"After Jesus said this, he looked toward heaven and prayed: 'Father, the time has come. Glorify your Son, that your Son may glorify you'"* (John 17:1). Our mission is to bring glory to the name of Jesus. *"All I have is yours, and all you have is mine. And glory has come to me through them"* (John 17:10). To do that, we have to grow in His glory: *"And we, who with unveiled faces all reflect the Lord's glory, are being transformed into his likeness with ever-increasing glory, which comes from the Lord, who is the Spirit"* (2 Corinthians 3:18).

In this global war, casualties are increasing and nations without prejudice are being attacked. People are being terrorized, regardless of their religion, political belief, location, or affiliations. It is a global war without borders. Active cells are everywhere. Psychological warfare is increasing with threats and intimidation that are paralyzing some and destabilizing freedom and economies. In 2015, there were hundreds of terrorist attacks in Africa, the Middle East, Israel, Asia, Europe, Australia, America, Canada, the Ukraine, and Korea, killing and wounding millions of people, not to mention the emotional trauma and other effects of war.

Families are being terrorized, displaced, and traumatized by enemies that cannot be easily detected. How can you fight who you do not know? How can you counterattack what you cannot see? The warfare and casualties are at several levels: physically with millions dying; mentally with deception and radicalization; emotionally with minds traumatized by fear; and spiritually as hopelessness is gripping hearts. Jesus Christ, however, is the Savior of our world and the answer to our world in crisis.

God intends to save His world. He suffered violence so that mankind can have peace: *"But He was wounded for our transgressions, He was bruised for our iniquities; the chastisement for our peace was upon Him, and by His stripes we are healed"* (Isaiah 53:5 NKJV). Jesus became poor (deprived Himself of Heaven's glory to live on an earth of dust) so that poverty can be broken. *"For you know the grace of our Lord Jesus Christ, that though he was rich, yet for your sakes he became poor, so that you through his poverty might become rich"* (2 Corinthians 8:9). He paid the price for our healing physically, mentally, emotionally, and spiritually.

The Bible teaches of times of darkness in our world that instigated moves of God through His people for cleansing, protection, restoration, justice, peace, and development. From the prophet Isaiah, we read, *"Arise, shine, for your light has come, and the glory of the Lord rises upon you.* **See, darkness covers the earth and thick darkness is over the peoples, but the Lord rises upon you and his glory appears over you.** *Nations will come to your light, and kings to the brightness of your dawn"* (Isaiah 60:1-3 emphasis added). In the midst of times of great darkness and fear in the world, the Lord rises upon His believing servants to glorify them to manifest His power and glory in and through them for salvation.

FROM GOD TO MOSES

"The Lord said, 'I have indeed seen the misery of my people in Egypt. I have heard them crying out because of their slave drivers, and I am concerned about their suffering. So I have come down to rescue them'" (Exodus 3:7-8). God glorified Moses and others to manifest His power and glory in and through them for the deliverance of slaves. God's glory in and through Moses forced Pharaoh to set over two million Jews free from slavery, stopped the murder of babies, restored the stolen resources of the Israelites—silver, gold, articles, and animals—and forced Pharaoh to give to the Israelites everything they needed to journey into their promised land.

FROM JESUS TO HIS CHURCH

> There will be signs in the sun, moon and stars. On the earth, nations will be in anguish and perplexity at the roaring and tossing of the sea. Men will faint from terror, apprehensive of what is coming on the world, for the heavenly bodies will be shaken. At that time they will see the Son of Man coming in a cloud with power and great glory. When these things begin to take place, stand up and lift up your heads, because your redemption is drawing near (Luke 21:25-28).

Note that Jesus will come down in a move of God to glorify His servants with His power and great glory.

We have a *cause*. We serve our King of glory, Savior of the world, and we are convinced that our world can only be saved by Jesus Christ. *"Salvation is found in no one else, for there is no other name under heaven given to men by which we must be saved"* (Acts 4:12). A move of God is promised: *"Therefore God exalted him [Jesus] to the highest place and gave him the name that is above every name, that at the name of Jesus every knee should bow, in heaven and on earth and under the earth, and every tongue confess that Jesus Christ is Lord, to the glory of God the Father"* (Philippians 2:9-11). Now is the time. CHAYIL glory is the manifested power and glory of our Lord Jesus Christ *in* and *through* His servants.

STRATEGY FOR MISSION INFUSION

1. **Prayer and intercession.** *"If my people, who are called by my name, will humble themselves and pray and seek my face and turn from their wicked ways, then will I hear from heaven and will forgive their sin and will heal their land"* (2 Chronicles 7:14). The prayer and intercession of believers in Christ will move the heart of God to release His plan of salvation of our world in our time. We are reminded of Apostle Paul's exhortation to the believers in the move of God during the time of the early Church: *"As God's fellow workers we urge you not to receive God's grace in vain. For he says, 'In the time of my favor I heard you, and in the day of salvation I helped you.' I tell you, now is the time of God's favor, now is the day of salvation"* (2 Corinthians 6:1-2). We also know that *now* is the day of salvation.

    Our prayer strategy as seen in 2 Chronicles 7:14:

    a. **"If my people, who are called by my name."** This move of God is to be led by the people of God with access to His throne of glory. It is for the glory of Jesus Christ to the glory of His Father:

"Therefore God exalted him to the highest place and gave him the name that is above every name, that at the name of Jesus every knee should bow, in heaven and on earth and under the earth, and every tongue confess that Jesus Christ is Lord, to the glory of God the Father" (Philippians 2:9-11).

b. **"Will humble themselves and pray."** Humility in unity. Denominations and networks in unity will create a release of God in our world that has never been seen before, *"The Lord said, 'If as one people speaking the same language they have begun to do this, then nothing they plan to do will be impossible for them'"* (Genesis 11:6). The disciples met in the upper room and prayed in humility and unity, and the heavens opened and a release of power and glory in them to flow through them as servants of Christ. They powerfully proved through miracles, signs, and wonders that Christ was alive *in* and *through* them so much so that they were called *Christians*, witnesses of Christ's resurrection power.

c. **"And seek my face."** Listen for *now* strategies for a *now* move of God. God kept the Israelites listening for what He was doing, when, how, and where. In the season of the wilderness, they were fed supernaturally with manna falling from the sky. However, in the promised land, there was a new move of God and God would feed them differently. *"So I have come down to rescue them from the hand of the Egyptians and to bring them up out of that land into a good and spacious land, a land flowing with milk and honey—the home of the Canaanites, Hittites, Amorites, Perizzites, Hivites and Jebusites"* (Exodus 3:7-8). Note, they had to find food and resources from the land, not from the sky. In this move of God, He would activate the covenant blessing with Abraham, to start from nothing to obtain land, start businesses, and grow into a strong nation.

God started a new move with new opportunities and industries: *"A land with wheat and barley, vines and fig trees, pomegranates, olive oil and honey; a land where bread will not be scarce and you will lack nothing; a land where the rocks are iron and you can dig copper out of the hills"* (Deuteronomy 8:8-9). When we seek God's face, we will see that He is seeing and hear what He is saying for new strategies for His Church and kingdom. In the promised land, there were many business opportunities with food supplies, commodities, housing developments, and promised prosperity for Israel as a strong kingdom. Israel came out from slavery to become a powerful kingdom of priests. Every move of God requires instructions from God as the commander of the move.

d. **"And turn from their wicked ways."** Repentance is always an integral part of every move of God. It is not *if* we sin, but *when* we sin individually and as a people. *"If we claim to be without sin, we deceive ourselves and the truth is not in us. If we confess our sins, he is faithful and just and will forgive us our sins and purify us from all unrighteousness. If we claim we have not sinned, we make him out to be a liar and his word has no place in our lives"* (1 John 1:8-10). The legal system of spiritual kingdoms, God's and Satan's, requires justification, covenants, and satisfaction. God has chosen to bind Himself to the legal system of the spiritual kingdoms and has given mankind the power of choice and the power to create and rule our world.

Jesus Christ, however, is the Defender of His Church and all believers in Him. The cross of Jesus Christ was the altar of God, with Jesus as the Lamb that was slain to satisfy all the sins of the world. Repentance is a powerful tool to free us from *all* sin. This is torment for Satan, who would like to inflict punishment on us every time we sin. That would be daily. More powerful, however, than the punishment of sin is the **mercy of God**. *"Mercy triumphs over judgment!"* (James 2:13). *"For he says to Moses, 'I will have mercy on whom I have mercy, and I will have compassion on whom I have compassion'"* (Roman 9:15).

God's agenda is to save all the people of the world, *"The Lord is not slack concerning His promise, as some count slackness, but is longsuffering toward us, not willing that any should perish but that all should come to repentance"* (2 Peter 3:9 NKJV). God patiently tries to save all people and has given us the power to repent for all failures, mistakes, and sins to receive His great mercy and forgiveness. God does not want to condemn anyone, regardless of their religion, beliefs, and deception. *"For God so loved the world that he gave his one and only Son, that whoever believes in him shall not perish but have eternal life. For God did not send his Son into the world to condemn the world, but to save the world through him"* (John 3:16-17).

e. **God will create a move to save our world.** His promise is threefold: 1. *"Then will I hear from heaven."* 2. *"I will forgive their sin."* 3. *"I will heal their land."*

2. ***Infusion with spiritual altars—building millions of spiritual altars to our King of glory in every nation.*** *"Now my eyes will be open and my ears attentive to the prayers offered in this place [wherever]"* (2 Chronicles 7:15). **Mission INFUSION** is "To *infuse* the CHAYIL glory of the Lord Jesus Christ in every heart, home, community, and nation." God's eyes will be open to see the places where He is lifted up and His ears open to the prayers and intercession of His humble servants of His mission. With millions of spiritual altars to our King of glory, the Lord Jesus Christ, in every heart (personal altar), home (family and home altars), school and workplace (community altars), church (altars of agreement and repentance), nation (national altars and altars of peace), the glory of the Lord Jesus Christ will infuse lives, communities, and nations with His love, mercy, forgiveness, hope, salvation, and transformation.

Every place where there is an altar to Jesus Christ, the blessing and power of the Lord will be evident, as it was in the home of Obed-Edom. *"The ark of the Lord remained in the house of Obed-Edom the Gittite for three months, and the Lord blessed him and his entire household"* (2 Samuel 6:11). The word *household* means family or business—all his ventures were blessed. Obed-Edom volunteered his home for God's ark, and God manifested His glory in every area of his life. Obed-Edom became famous, and everyone knew why he was so blessed: *"Now King David was told, 'The Lord has blessed the household of Obed-Edom and everything he has, because of the ark of God.' So David went down and brought up the ark of God from the house of Obed-Edom to the City of David with rejoicing'"* (2 Samuel 6:12).

The powerful presence of Jesus Christ in every community and nation will grow in manifestation of His glory to topple the powerful presence of evil that is now seeking to dominate our world. The choice we have is to either permit the manifested power of evil to continue, which is now tormenting, terrorizing, and threatening our world, or to allow Jesus Christ, our King of glory, to manifest His glory in and through His servants to save our world with His manifested glory of mercy, grace, restoration, and transformation of lives, communities, and nations.

3. ***Infusion with spiritual hotspots—millions of CHAYIL Power Groups as spiritual hotspots in every nation.*** A *hotspot* is described as a place of significant activity, a small region with hot temperature, a place where a fire is likely to start or has been burning, area of volcanic activity, a place for wireless access to internet connections. A hotspot has access to the clouds for extensive range of information, resources, and services.

A **spiritual hotspot** has access to the heavens and the throne of glory of our Lord God Almighty for power, authority, glory, resources, miracles, angelic help, protection, revelation, instruction, direction, inspiration, and influence.

A *CHAYIL Power Group* (CPG) has three or more members meeting regularly for worship, prayer, Bible study, and growing in spiritual gifts, using Jesus' model for values and intentional growth in CHAYIL pillars, peer coaching, collective wisdom from the group, accountability, care, fellowship, building spiritual altars to our King of glory, and motivating each other for holistic prosperity. It is like a cell group but with additional components (the *CHAYIL factor*). It is called a CHAYIL Power Group as it involves the law of synergy: *"How could one man chase a thousand, or two put ten thousand to flight, unless their Rock had sold them, unless the Lord had given them up?"* (Deuteronomy 32:30). The power of God, the power of numbers, and collective faith in unity and intention create the atmosphere where all things are possible.

Examples of CHAYIL Power Groups:

Jesus, Peter, James, John: *"After six days Jesus took with him Peter, James and John the brother of James, and led them up a high mountain by themselves"* (Matthew 17:1). *"He did not let anyone follow him except Peter, James and John the brother of James"* (Mark 5:37). *"They went to a place called Gethsemane, and Jesus said to his disciples, 'Sit here while I pray.' He took Peter, James and John along with him, and he began to be deeply distressed and troubled"* (Mark 14:32-33). Jesus strategically had a more intimate and private relationship, held discussions, and performed miracles with His CHAYIL Power Group. With this powerful group in unity and trust, He performed miracles that did not involve crowds and the other disciples. Unity, trust, and agreement releases power.

Daniel, Shadrach, Meshach and Abednego: *"Moreover, at Daniel's request the king appointed Shadrach, Meshach and Abednego administrators over the province of Babylon, while Daniel himself remained at the royal court"* (Daniel 2:49). These four Hebrew boys grew up as slaves in Babylon who intentionally resisted becoming radicalized Babylonians or engaging in idolatry. They supported and motivated each other in prayer, encouragement, and wisdom.

They went through great trials that God used to manifest His great glory in Babylon, and the kings eventually bowed to Jehovah, the Most High: *"Nebuchadnezzar then approached the opening of the blazing furnace and shouted, 'Shadrach, Meshach and Abednego, servants of the Most High God, come out! Come here!'"* (Daniel 3:26). Unity, trust, and agreement releases power.

4. ***Infusion of CHAYIL glory.*** It is called CHAYIL glory because of its intention and effect. CHAYIL glory means powerful, kinetic, active, strategic, moving, manifesting glory in and through believing servants. Christ, our Hope of glory, can be dormant glory in Christians—not seen, shown, or heard. Jesus understood this principle: *"After Jesus said this, he looked toward heaven and prayed: 'Father, the time has come. Glorify your Son, that your Son may glorify you'"* (John 17:1). Moses, David, Elijah, David, and the disciples of Jesus manifested CHAYIL glory for the glory of God, the Source. CHAYIL glory is covenant glory. God glorifies His servants so that His servants can glorify Him. We cannot glorify God without His glory.

Spiritual altars will be built by faith to intentionally infuse that home, place, community, and nation with the manifested glory of the Lord Jesus Christ, *"That at the name of Jesus every knee should bow, in heaven and on earth and under the earth, and every tongue confess that Jesus Christ is Lord, to the glory of God the Father"* (Philippians 2:10-11). CHAYIL glory is the manifested power and glory of our Lord Jesus Christ *in* and *through* His servants. Ordinary believers will be filled with the power and glory of our Lord Jesus Christ to flow *in* and *through* them, as He did through men and women of faith throughout the ages. God's harvests will be trained to loose and gather harvest of people, land, and resources. It is a movement of transformation of lives, communities, and nations. Training will include prayer, evangelism, land acquisition, and resources.

With the infusion of the glory of the Lord Jesus Christ in communities, demonic powers will bow and be neutralized, and hearts and lives will become free to unite to the true and living Savior of the world, Jesus Christ, to intentionally displace evil principalities in dominion and replace them with Jesus Christ as Savior and Lord.

The Power of His Glory (The Dagon Principle)

> After the Philistines had captured the ark of God, they took it from Ebenezer to Ashdod. Then they carried the ark into Dagon's temple and set it beside Dagon. When the people of Ashdod rose early the next day, there was Dagon, fallen on his face on the ground before the ark of the Lord! They took Dagon and put him back in his place. But the following morning when they rose, there was Dagon, fallen on his face on the ground before the ark of the Lord! His head and hands had been broken off and were lying on the threshold; only his body remained (1 Samuel 5:1-4).

Displace to replace. When we infuse hearts, homes, communities, and nations with the glory of our Lord Jesus Christ, demonic powers automatically will fall and lose their heads (authority) and hands (influence). *"Therefore God exalted him to the highest place and gave him the name that is above every name, that at the name of Jesus every knee should bow, in heaven and on earth and under the earth, and every tongue confess that Jesus Christ is Lord, to the glory of God the Father"* (Philippians 2:9-11). With intention, we know what we are doing, why we are doing it, where strategically, when in timing, and how, with expected results.

5. ***Missions and community outreach.*** Training will include prayer, evangelism, land acquisition, and resources. Most believers are already in involved in loosing and reaping a harvest of people with prayer, evangelism, global missions, and outreach. However, strategic intercession and training in harvest of land and resources will be added.

6. ***Activating influential leaders.*** Influential and government leaders will be encourage to intentionally build spiritual altars to our King of glory in communities and nations. Jesus will rule in nations where He is invited by influential leaders.

> Then Noah built an altar to the Lord and, taking some of all the clean animals and clean birds, he sacrificed burnt offerings on it. The Lord smelled the pleasing aroma and said in his heart: "Never again will I curse the ground because of man, even though every inclination of his heart is evil from childhood. And never again will I destroy all living creatures, as I have done" (Genesis 8:20-21).

Noah's altar was powerful to motivate the heart of God to make a vow to preserve humanity and all living creatures on the earth. Influential men and women of companies, rulers, political leaders, and societal leaders have the legal authority to establish the kingdom of God in their areas and territories.

7. ***Media.*** Media is a weapon of mass deliverance and transformation of lives. It creates synergetic spiritual warfare against the prince or ruler of the kingdom of the air. *"In which you used to live when you followed*

the ways of this world and of the ruler of the kingdom of the air, the spirit who is now at work in those who are disobedient" (Ephesians 2:2). Satan is also called *"The prince of the power of the air"* (Ephesians 2:2 NKJV). Revelation of truth is powerful to set captives free from deception, oppression, and all the vices of the devil. Media, technology, and other tools are used to share information so others can join the CHAYIL Glory Movement of **Mission INFUSION**, "To infuse the CHAYIL glory of the Lord Jesus Christ in every heart, home, community, and nation." *"For the earth will be filled with the knowledge of the glory of the Lord, as the waters cover the sea"* (Habakkuk 2:14).

Together we are a mighty CHAYIL army who will pray, serve, go, share, and show forth the glory of the Lord Jesus Christ everywhere. *"After the Lord Jesus had spoken to them, he was taken up into heaven and he sat at the right hand of God. Then the disciples went out and preached everywhere, and the Lord worked with them and confirmed his word by the signs that accompanied it"* (Mark 16:19-20).

Join the movement. Let us pray, believe, and receive fresh outpouring of the power and glory of the Lord Jesus Christ in us to flow through us as we serve His glory. Like the disciples, let us be transformed into the likeness of Christ for His ever-increasing glory. Let us share with others, recruit others, and train others to grow in CHAYIL glory to fill the earth with the manifested power and glory of the Lord Jesus Christ. *"From the days of John the Baptist until now, the kingdom of heaven has been forcefully advancing, and forceful men lay hold of it"* (Matthew 11:12). *"And the glory of the Lord will be revealed, and all mankind **together** will see it. For the mouth of the Lord has spoken"* (Isaiah 40:5).

Together as the CHAYIL army of EL CHAYIL, Lord of armies, King of glory, Lord of wealth we believe and agree: *"The earth shall be filled with the glory of the Lord"* (Numbers 14:21). We must intentionally grow in the wineskin of Jesus in the CHAYIL pillars to nurture His glory in and through us. *"And Jesus grew in wisdom and statue, and in favor with God and men"* (Luke 2:52). God's will for us is that we grow in His strength, power, and glory. *"And we, who with unveiled faces all reflect the Lord's glory, are being transformed into his likeness with ever-increasing glory, which comes from the Lord, who is the Spirit"* (2 Corinthians 3:18). Let us pray, believe, and receive fresh outpouring of glory. Together and by God's grace and glory, we will serve to transform lives, communities, and nations and loose and reap God's harvest of people, land, and resources. God has heard our cries for mercy, freedom, and salvation. The answer is in one name—*Jesus*. CHAYIL glory is the manifested power and glory of our Lord Jesus Christ in and through servants like you. Together we can.

PRAYERS FOR CHAYIL GLORY

Jesus prayed, *"Father, the time has come. Glorify your Son, that your Son may glorify you"* (John 17:1).

Moses prayed, *"Show me your glory"* (Exodus 33:18).

David prayed, *"Be exalted, O God, above the heavens; let your glory be over all the earth"* (Psalm 57:11).

We pray, "Father, the time has come. Glorify your servants, that your servants may glorify you."

Angels declare, "Mission INFUSION accomplished!" *"And they were calling to one another: "Holy, holy, holy is the Lord Almighty; the whole earth is full of his glory"* (Isaiah 6:3).

Arise, shine, for your light has come, and the glory of the Lord rises upon you. See, darkness covers the earth and thick darkness is over the peoples, but the Lord rises upon you and his glory appears over you. Nations will come to your light, and kings to the brightness of your dawn (Isaiah 60:1-3). Amen!

In the words of Jesus Christ, our King of glory: *"At that time they will see the Son of Man coming in a cloud with power and great glory. When these things begin to take place, stand up and lift up your heads, because your redemption is drawing near"* (Luke 21:27-28). CHAYIL glory is the manifested power and glory of our Lord Jesus Christ *in* and *through* His servants. Serve His glory, and His glory will serve you. EL CHAYIL, Lord of armies, King of glory, Lord of wealth, has already won the battle for you. When you take care of His business, He will take care of yours: *"But seek first his kingdom and his righteousness, and all these things will be given to you as well"* (Matthew 6:33).

We are a CHAYIL "David Generation": *"Day after day men came to help David, until he had a great army, like the army of God"* (1 Chronicles 12:22).

CHAPTER 16

The CHAYIL Glory Movement

And they were calling to one another: "Holy, holy, holy is the Lord Almighty; the whole earth is full of his glory" (Isaiah 6:3).

In the CHAYIL Glory Movement, God is enhancing, empowering, and engaging His Church and believing servants as an elite force to join EL CHAYIL, Lord of armies, King of glory, Lord of wealth, to display His glory as Savior of our world. The mission of Jesus is to save lives, advance His kingdom, build His Church, and fill the earth with His glory. *"And the glory of the Lord will be revealed, and all mankind together will see it. For the mouth of the Lord has spoken"* (Isaiah 40:5). In this movement, God's harvest will be loosed and reaped in three areas: people, land, and resources. Jesus Christ is our Lord of harvest.

God's Church continues to grow in revelation, maturity, and power for a great showdown against the evil principalities that are dominating our world with torment, terror, corruption, violence, and poverty. The **CHAYIL factor** is revelation for greater transformation of lives, community, and nations. It involves strategic spiritual warfare with God, who is sending us with a message to evil principalities to "loose His harvest of people, land, and resources into His Church and kingdom!" This loosing of harvest is like in the days of Moses, Joshua, and David, with mighty exploits. God's believing servants, therefore, have to be prepared and positioned as His harvesters.

Jesus Christ is our Lord of the harvest: *"Then he said to his disciples, 'The harvest is plentiful but the workers are few. Ask the Lord of the harvest, therefore, to send out workers into his harvest field'"* (Matthew 9:37-38).

The CHAYIL Glory Movement includes building spiritual altars to Jesus Christ; engaging in strategic intercession; creating CHAYIL Power Groups as spiritual hotspots; using Jesus' model for values and intentional growth in CHAYIL pillars; loosing and reaping harvest of people, land, and resources; and applying the CHAYIL factor to serve networks and churches for greater unified results. *"For the earth will be filled with the knowledge of the glory of the Lord, as the waters cover the sea"* (Habakkuk 2:14). Training will include prayer, evangelism, and acquisition of land and resources.

In this move of God, we are understanding the kind of manifested glory that God is displaying in and through His servants *now*. His manifested glory through Moses was in great authority even over nature; it had the influence to deliver millions of slaves and perform incredible signs and wonders that made God famous in surrounding nations.

His manifested glory through Joshua in the promised land was different. No more manna and quail from Heaven. Joshua was in successful battles to possess more and more land, and the Israelites had to plant for food and dig wells for water. Israel was glorified for establishment and development for resources.

God's manifested glory through David was different. David was not only successful in battles and land acquisition, but also with great wealth for the establishment of Israel as a prosperous, strong nation and kingdom. David's glory included great alliances with kings and kingdoms and incredible wealth.

God's manifested glory through the disciples of Jesus was in saving thousands of people, launching Christianity, infusing nations with the gospel of the kingdom, and performing great miracles, signs, and wonders. Worships services were in homes and synagogues. The manifesting glory of God in and through His servants of His mission is always according to the agenda of His mission in that time and season. Now us.

Among David's CHAYIL (mighty) army in the great move of God were the men of Issachar: *"who understood the times and knew what Israel should do—200 chiefs, with all their relatives under their command"* (1 Chronicles 12:32). Now us. We must now understand the times in this age of modern society in the twenty-first century, what the church should do, and the involvement of all ages, cultures, kingdoms, and societies. We learn the principles of God's journey with humanity, His starting afresh with Abraham, and His evolution with the Church of Jesus Christ. We are not the early Church, and therefore the Church now should be a more matured and growing Church in the ever-increasing glory of Christ.

Every move of God has common factors such as prayer, obedient and passionate servants, faith, unity, and strategy. In the CHAYIL Glory Movement, the CHAYIL factor is used to serve churches, networks, and ministries for a unified approach for greater and quicker results. *"Growing greater quicker for greater results."*

THE CHAYIL FACTOR FOR CELL GROUPS

* Intentional growth of each member with collective wisdom and coaching from the group.
* Using Jesus' model for values and intentional growth in CHAYIL pillars, Luke 2:52.
* Building spiritual altars to our King of glory.
* Motivating each other for holistic prosperity in all areas of our lives.

THE CHAYIL FACTOR FOR PRAYER MEETINGS

1. Understanding kingdom dynamics and the legal system of the spirit world for mediation, negotiations, contracts, covenants, etc.
2. Building spiritual altars to our King of glory:
   * Altars for intercession
   * Community altars
   * National altars
   * Altars of repentance
   * Altars of peace

THE CHAYIL FACTOR FOR HOLISTIC GROWTH

CHAYIL Pillars are worship, wisdom, power, honor, favor, wealth, and influence and describe our intent to grow like Jesus and with godly core values. The Bible describes the intentional growth of Jesus: *"And Jesus grew in **wisdom** and stature, and in **favor** with God and men"* (Luke 2:52 emphasis added). Amplified, this verse can read, *"And Jesus grew in wisdom [understanding, revelation, sense, insight] and stature [**power**, **honor**, maturity, respect], and in favor with God [**worship**, prayer, humility, obedience] and favor with men [prominence, **wealth, influence**]."* The words in bold form the CHAYIL pillars, including wealth, where we see how our Heavenly Father powerfully motivated wise men to bring great wealth to His Son as a child. *"And when they had come into the house, they saw the young Child with Mary His mother, and fell down and worshiped Him. And when they had opened their treasures, they* *presented gifts to Him: gold, frankincense, and myrrh"* (Matthew 2:11 NKJV). God is *Provider* for His mission.

The CHAYIL pillars describe the wineskin for the glory of Jesus Christ as seen in the way He grew from a baby to a man. As we intentionally seek to grow like Jesus, His character, power, and glory will manifest in and through us. God became man and lived on earth in the flesh of Jesus to show us how ordinary believing servants of God can be like God on earth. As Christian believers, our aim is to be like Christ and serve Him in His mission to save the world, advance His kingdom, build His Church, and fill the earth with His glory. Jesus Christ is the Hope of our world: *"To them God has chosen to make known among the Gentiles the glorious riches of this mystery, which is Christ in you, the hope of glory"* (Colossians 1:27).

AGENDA OF A CHAYIL POWER GROUP MEETING

* ***Welcome, prayer (worship), introduction***
* ***One-word check in.*** Each person is asked to use one word to describe how they are feeling. It is good for you to be real so that others can either inspire you when needed or celebrate you and your testimony. If you are feeling challenged or if you have an issue, you can receive prayer or collective wisdom (ideas and experiences) from other members. *"Growing greater together."*
* ***One-word explanation.*** Each person will explain their one word check in for celebration, prayer, or peer coaching (if desired).
* ***Peer coaching.*** Peer coaching is when a member of the CPG share an issue about which they would like to receive ideas, wisdom, and strategies from the

experiences of other members in the group. Everyone will get opportunities to share or receive coaching from others. This is a great way to receive coaching and mentorship from others.

* ***Interactive discussion*** of CHAYIL Daily Inspiration or Bible study.
* ***Training in CHAYIL pillars: Worship, Wisdom, Power, Honor, Favor, Wealth, Influence.*** Choose a pillar for discussion. How are you intentionally growing in that pillar? Share at next session—growth for accountability.
* ***One-word check out.*** Before conclusion of the meeting, a one-word check out will describe how each person is feeling after the group meeting.
* ***Prayer.*** At the end of the CPG, an altar of intercession with the power of agreement is created to pray for the needs of members, family, ministry, business, nation, etc. Altar of intercession (Exodus 17:10-13); power of agreement (Matthew 18:18-20).
* ***Fellowship.***

Each CHAYIL Power Group will add dynamics according to the people in the group and their desired growth.

Location of CHAYIL Power Groups: home, church, school, workplace, online, Skype, telephone, media, local, or global.

The Word of the Lord for us in this season is, *"Arise, shine, for your light has come, and the glory of the Lord rises upon you. See, darkness covers the earth and thick darkness is over the peoples, but the Lord rises upon you and his glory appears over you"* (Isaiah 60:1-2). Jesus Christ has come down: *"At that time they will see the Son of Man coming in a cloud with **power** and **great glory**. When these things begin to take place, stand up and lift up your heads, because your redemption is drawing near"* (Luke 21:27-28 emphasis added).

Notice that Jesus describes His glory as great, which in the Hebrew language is CHAYIL.

CHAYIL glory is the manifested power and glory of the Lord Jesus Christ *in* and *through* His servants. Together, let us pray, serve, go, give, and agree with the declaration of Heaven, *"Holy, holy, holy is the Lord Almighty; the whole earth is full of his glory"* (Isaiah 6:3).

For more information about Pat Francis Ministries and other resources available from Pat Francis, please email or call:

Email: chayil@patfrancis.org
Phone: 905 566 1084
Fax: 905 566 1154

www.patfrancis.org
www.kingdomcovenant.ca
www.chayilglory.org